THE HIPSTER EFFECT

THE HIPSTER EFFECT

HOW THE RISING TIDE OF
INDIVIDUALITY IS CHANGING
EVERYTHING WE KNOW ABOUT LIFE,
WORK AND THE PURSUIT
OF HAPPINESS

SOPHY BOT

The Hipster Effect: How the Rising Tide of Individuality is Changing
Everything We Know about Life, Work and the Pursuit of Happiness

ISBN-13: 978-0615629261

ISBN-10: 0615629261

Edited by Rick Raguso

Front cover, back cover and section illustrations by
João Raposo, Fullking.com

Infographics by Made of People, Madeofpeople.org

thehipstereffect.com

For my mom.

Thank you for letting me do my own thing
(no matter how bizarre that sometimes seemed).

"Insist on yourself; never imitate."

—*Ralph Waldo Emerson, 1841*

TABLE OF CONTENTS

Chapter 1.2: Punk is Dead. Long Live Punk.

The traditional notion of the subculture has all but disappeared as society has become more and more fragmented. Timelines have shrunk between the creation of a trend and its worldwide propagation, leading subcultures to become microcultures and introducing us to more ways of living than ever available in human history.

Chapter 1.3: The Rise of the Hipster, the Fall of the Rebel.

Western society has been steadily shedding its formality for over half a century. The rise of the casual aesthetic has, in turn, made us more accepting of even the most extreme forms of self-expression. This societal progression has led the rebel to evolve into its inevitable successor: the hipster.

2...THE INTERNET HAS CHANGED US

Chapter 2.1: Rule 34

The internet has fueled the globalization of modern society, exposing us to more opinions and options than ever before available. Navigating the internet and directly pursuing our interests has changed the way we experience our culture. We may all play by the same *how,* but we now want to choose for ourselves the *what.*

Chapter 2.2: 1,000,000 Strong for Anything

Our social ties are no longer limited by geography. The sheer size and scope of the internet allows us to find like-minded people whether they're halfway around the world or right next door. Not only are there others out there like us; we now have the ability to find and interact with them directly.

3 . . . WE'VE CHANGED OUR IDENTITIES

The ability to experiment with online profiles as avenues of self-expression has never, since its inception, been relegated to youth. Identity play has now become a lifelong endeavor, whether online or off. Unique self-expression is no longer limited to specific age groups or subcultures. These days, it's just the way of the world.

4 ... THE LINE BETWEEN LIFE AND WORK IS CHANGING

Now that both work and play have a huge online component and technology has matured enough to allow the internet to be with us at all times, previous barriers separating life from work are steadily eroding. Our business and social lives are mixing, but the rules for interaction have yet to be set.

Today's young workforce wants to succeed based on skills, not job longevity. While many view these younger employees as lazy, the truth is that they simply have a different way of viewing the workplace. Companies need to adapt to take advantage of employees' new skill sets rather than trying to fit digital pegs into analog holes.

A growing body of studies has demonstated that we are both happier and more productive when allowed to choose our own schedules and to take occasional breathers from our work. As it turns out, allowing some distraction and humor into the workplace ultimately leads to higher-quality work and happier employees. Win/win.

5 ... CONCLUSION

Chapter 5.1: Hipster? I Hardly Know Her!   151

What we call a hipster is just somebody self-expressing in a way that our society has otherwise come to accept. Rather than continuing our knee-jerk hatred of all things hipster, what we ought to do is take advantage of the freedom of choice that is the true heart of the hipster phenomenon—in other words: it's time to embrace the hipster effect.

O . . . INTRODUCTION

HOMO HIPSTERUS

Nobody can be sure who uttered the word first, but soon enough it grew wings and fluttered from ear to ear, from loft to loft, from email to email. Was it started by J., the resident capitalist of the building, always trying to find some way to finance his newest artwork? Or perhaps it was first uttered by H., the owner of the art gallery in the basement whose personal work was wholly focused on America's founding fathers (despite his Japanese heritage)? Could it have been M., the absurdist street performer known for his wild beard and white dress, a man who once met my mother wearing nothing but red body paint and a large Swiss flag?

Who was it at 345 Eldert Street that first announced, "secede?"

The time: July 2007.

The place: A sewing factory-turned-squat house-turned-loft building in the far reaches of Bushwick, Brooklyn, home to 100+ artists and creative types too poor to live in either Manhattan or nearby Williamsburg.

The idea: Find a group of investors to purchase the building, allowing the artist residents to live and work within the space at below market rates. In other words, "to secede from Brooklyn in protest of 'destructive economic forces.'"[1]

The people: Call them hipsters. Everybody else did.

I had left town for the summer that year but was a resident of 3-4-5 (as the building was lovingly nicknamed) both before and after the secession attempt. I watched from afar as the passionate cries of my friends got shot down by blogs and by word on the street, calling the newly formed *United Studios of Eldert* nothing more than a bunch of whiny hipsters. Their efforts were mocked and their idea ultimately failed, but the one part everybody seemed to miss was that, despite all of the hipster-aimed naysaying so pervasive in the media at the time and since, here was a group of people sincerely pursuing their beliefs. This was hardly "the end of Western civilization," as hipsters were once described in a scathing article by AdBusters.[2] This was not a group of people "with nothing to defend, uphold or even embrace." These people were not "human filth"[3] or "repulsive,"[4] as hipsters have variously been termed. These were bohemians, pure and simple, and they were trying to make a stand. Unfortunately, once they were hit with the h-word, they didn't stand a chance.

"If you live in a metropolitan city... you start to notice that there are as many hipsters infesting your region as there are cockroaches... The only main

difference between the two is that you can kill a
cockroach legally."

—*Kerry Da Silva, blogger*[5]

Definitions of the hipster range from the pragmatic to the
malicious, and rarely do any two writers agree. Most articles
about hipsters provide little more than a laundry list of
traits and interests, a list that in itself changes with every
author's personal opinion of just what a hipster is. Fashion
items are mentioned (thick-rimmed glasses, skinny jeans,
trucker hats), as are preferred modes of transportation (fixed
gear bicycle, Vespa, used sedan), favored beverages (PBR,
Miller High Life, locally brewed organic coffee) and neighbor-
hoods of choice (Williamsburg, Brooklyn; Silver Lake, LA;
Berkeley, San Francisco). Some articles list surefire phrases used
to identify the hipster:

"If, when asked what you do for a living, you reply,
'I'm an artist,' you're a hipster."[6]

"'Their first album was better' (this is actually the
hipster mating call)"[7]

"'I don't believe in labels.' (I do and mine is
'hipster.')"[8]

In fact, the only two things that all of these articles seem to
agree on is that (1) hipsters really like Pabst Blue Ribbon and
(2) hipsters tend to be highly educated. So why all the hipster
hate?

BOHEMIA 2.0

When I first moved into 3-4-5, I felt as though I was transported back in time to some era of *cool* I thought had long since ceased to exist. Residents would gather in the hallways and on the rooftop, discussing their latest creative projects and brewing up collaborations. On the weekends you could hit four parties without ever stepping outside of the front door. The freight elevator served as an ever-replenishing pile of free (if worn) goods, stacked and scoured by residents on a daily basis. I met people who worked in the circus, people who played with famous musicians, people who had gallery showings that very evening, would I like to stop by? Having just quit a fairly lucrative Midtown job—not to mention having just emerged from a 5-year marriage and accompanying Upper East Side yuppie lifestyle—3-4-5 showed me that the New York underground was not only still alive and kicking, it was an actual scene and it was surprisingly accepting of cultural foreigners like me. This was bohemia and creative Mecca wrapped up into one, with inspiration and ramen perpetually on hand.

You see, I was never cool myself. Growing up in and around Russian New York, the Beastie Boys track "No Sleep Till Brooklyn" sorely confused me, as I could see no reason to be *that* passionate about Brighton Beach and Sheepshead Bay. Williamsburg was a revelation. The year I discovered it was 2006, long after the modern hipster had been born and supposedly died out. It was a word that I began to hear more of with every month that I stayed in Bushwick. It would take only six months of living there for people to start labeling *me* a hipster. And having gone from yuppie to hipster in less than a year, I can tell you that I was more than a little confused.

As I sit here and write this five years later, it seems that I am both more and less confused about the whole hipster enigma than I was when I first stumbled into it. Since my days at 3-4-5, I have spent extended periods of time with so-called hipsters in Montreal, Lisbon, Berlin, San Francisco and Denver, all of which has changed my worldview and my sense of style. If you saw me walking down the street these days, you'd probably call me a hipster without thinking twice. Rather than conforming to the yuppie office aesthetic as I once did, I now wear clothing that I feel expresses my personality. I make my living creatively through freelancing and consulting work and spend my spare time on writing, art and music projects. There is PBR in my refrigerator and I own a pair of Wayfarer sunglasses, not because I'm trying to fit in with the hipster scene, but because PBR is cheap and I happen to like that particular pair of shades. Unfortunately, if you're like most people, some part of you would hate me the second you saw me, for no reason other than how I was dressed and the associations that caused.

GOD SAVE THE HIPSTER

"Hipsters are a subculture of men and women typically in their 20's and 30's that value independent thinking, counter-culture, progressive politics,

an appreciation of art and indie-rock, creativity, intelligence, and witty banter."
—*Urban Dictionary*[9]

"Hipsters are the friends who sneer when you cop to liking Coldplay… Everything about them is exactingly constructed to give off the vibe that they just don't care."
—*Dan Fletcher, Time Magazine*[10]

When it comes to hipsters, it seems there's just no winning. While the occasional definition points out the positive traits, most are far more likely to skew towards the venomous. In the popular media, hipsters have come to represent everything that is perceived as terrible about modern society. They're portrayed as being obsessed with consumer goods, being extremely judgmental, being arrogant, and generally lacking in substance. Hipsters are said to be whiny and entitled, big kids who are used to getting what they want, when they want. They are seen as caring about cool and nothing *but* cool. They're also seen as being ubiquitous and unstoppable. Having just one of the dozens of traits ascribed to the hipster seems to make you one yourself, all other traits notwithstanding. Being an actual artist doesn't help your cause either, nor does having actual beliefs and views, as my friends at 3-4-5 discovered back in 2007. So I ask once again: why all the hipster hate?

Just as Parisian bohemians were shunned as signaling the end of all things right and good back in the 1840s, hipsters are now derided as a derivative and substance-less knock-off of a greater era. The label is freely applied, escalating to an everybody-hates-everybody-else game of widespread hipster hate. No redeeming qualities are ever given, nor is any single definition ever agreed upon. We seem to have built up all of our hatred based on certain consumer goods that we associate with a certain aesthetic and a certain attitude. We judge the hipsters for judging us, quid pro quo, ad infinitum. It's time to end the cycle and take a look at what it really means to be a "hipster" in the modern, internet-connected world.

SUBMITTED FOR YOUR APPROVAL

What follows in these pages is an examination of how we ended up at this particular point in our cultural—and subcultural—evolution. Look closely and you'll see that hipsters are nothing more than a product of the natural development of our society. The knee-jerk hatred that surrounds hipsters betrays a deeper lack of understanding of who they are and where they came from. By examining key cultural trends, we'll take a look at the inner workings of typical hipster behaviors to better understand their actual motivations and desires.

I'd like to be clear that this book is not technically about hipsters. This is a book about identity and the social construct. Over the past few decades, the world has transformed at a faster rate than ever before in human history. Western society has splintered along a million invisible divides, and we are only now beginning to grasp just how different an internet-connected culture really is. The hipster is no more than an archetype, the hatred of which largely adds up to hating ourselves for who we've become.

This book is divided into four main sections. Section 1 deals with how subcultures have evolved throughout the last century. It explains how we've come to divide ourselves into smaller and smaller groups and how society as a whole has become more casual and more accepting of different lifestyles. Section 2 goes into the internet-connected modern life, providing a description of how the internet has changed the way we navigate the world around us. Section 3 covers the role of identity in the creation of the self, and how that role has changed dramatically over the last fifty years. From social networks to ubiquitous customization and design, our identities are personally constructed in a way that is historically unprecedented. Section 4 talks about how the traditional wall between home life and work life has been steadily eroding, and how both employees and employers can make the best of cultural trends and scientific studies to rethink that wall while benefiting from both increased happiness and productivity. Finally, a conclusion chapter will return to the concept of the hipster, tying together all of the information presented to debunk the traditionally derisive notion of the modern hipster, with the hope of diffusing some of those hateful reactions directed towards people with an innate affinity for skinny jeans.

And so, as the hipsters might say: Let's get this party started.

1 . . . SUBCULTURES
HAVE CHANGED

I, REBEL

"Once, during Prohibition, I was forced to live for
days on nothing but food and water."
—*W. C. Fields, comedian*

CALL IT GETTING LOADED. Oiled. Jingled. Fried. Bleary-eyed.
Under the table. Loaded to the muzzle. Lit up like a
Christmas tree. Whatever you call it, it stopped at the stroke
of midnight on January 16th, 1920 as the Volstead Act—
better known as the Prohibition Era—went into effect, and
Americans everywhere were suddenly left without water in
their wells. Funerals were held in honor of John Barleycorn,
comedians found a whole new shtick to work off of ("You
may kiss the bride." "I'll need a drink for that!"[11]), and all
across the United States moonshine distilleries quietly hummed
into life. It was the start of a new decade, the Roaring Twenties,
the Jazz Age, the Boom Era, and Prohibition wasn't the only
thing radically different about this one.

With World War I now behind it and the deadly Influenza
pandemic finally over, the United States awoke to a robust

economy and sweeping cultural changes. Cars hit the road en masse, their numbers ballooning from 6.8 million in 1919 to a whopping 122 million by 1929.[12] For the first time in the country's history, more Americans were now living in cities than in rural areas. It was the decade that saw the introduction of the first commercial radio programming and the popularization of "talkies" over the previously pervasive silent films. The average American's workweek was reduced from 60 hours to 48,[13] and the average woman's domestic chores were greatly simplified by the arrival of household appliances and ready-made breads, soups, cereals and other foods that traditionally needed to be cooked from scratch. Machine-manufactured apparel made its way into stores and working-class women were suddenly able to dress in facsimiles of the outfits previously reserved for the wealthy and famous. It was the era of the speakeasy, those clandestine bars used to sling hooch and "white lightning" to the alcohol-deprived American public, away from the watching eyes of the older generation. Americans had more time on their hands than ever before, pop culture had only just been born, and the availability of mass-produced goods was beginning to grow with every year, leaving the conditions ripe for the birth of America's first great subculture: the flappers.

The flappers were a group of independent, vivacious women set on a course of exploring all those facets of life that had previously been forbidden. In an age when showing ankles was considered scandalous, these women bared their knees. Long hair was viewed as a woman's crowning glory; they cut theirs off into short, bobbed hairdos. Drinking was illegal and female smoking, disgraceful; these women did both, and they did them often. The popularization of the automobile provided a mobile venue for their newfound (and highly shunned) hobbies of "petting" and visiting "Lovers' Lane." Speakeasies provided further privacy. In the words of Clara Bow, one of the most famous movie stars of the time and a widely publicized flapper, "In my era, we had individuality. We did as we pleased. We stayed up late. We dressed the way we wanted… Today they're sensible and end up with better health—but we had more fun."[14]

The timing of Ms. Bow's quote was 1951, and by then everything had changed. The Roaring Twenties came to a grinding halt on October 24th, 1929 as the stock market crashed, America entered the Great Depression, the globe entered World War II, and the conditions that had made the Flapper era possible came tumbling down all around. Suddenly finding themselves struggling for food, shelter and survival, Americans simply had no time to question the status quo. Not, that is, until the late 1950s.

THERE WILL BE HIPPIES

At first it seemed like everything was coming up roses. The decade between 1950 and 1960 brought with it a booming economy, affordable home ownership in the newly established suburbs, more cars on the roads, more mass-produced goods across all spheres of life, affordable college educations and an overall higher standard of living than ever seen before. It was the era of the television, with pop culture being broadcast into 87% of homes by 1960[15] and politics making its way into John Q. Public's living room as the first ever TV-broadcast debate brought John F. Kennedy and Richard M. Nixon into black-and-white life. There was increased freedom in behavior and speech throughout society and by all accounts, the new generation coming of age should have been thrilled.

They weren't.

> The students' basic demand is a demand to be heard,
> to be considered.
> —*Port Huron Statement*[16]

The hippie subculture was born against the background of the Vietnam War and the newfound affluence of the older generation. The youth wanted no part in the materialism being touted by their parents and so they rejected popular mainstream notions to concoct their own way of living. If men's hair was meant to be short, the hippies grew theirs long. If clothing was meant to be drab and formal, the hippies went for bright patterns and flowers in their hair. If 9-to-5 jobs were the only way to make a respectable living, the hippies went for spontaneity and spur-of-the-moment travel. And if war was the name of the game, the hippies would instead make love.

A new culture had come into being in parallel with the mainstream version being lived by their parents, only this was not a culture separated by geographic boundaries, but by modes of dress, slang, self-expression, art and music. Famous hippies encouraged a relaxed view of life, with Timothy Leary telling kids to "drop out—of high school, college, grad school, junior executive,"[17] and Abby Hoffman urging them to "get out of school, quit your job."[18] The more dedicated members of the subculture retreated into the woods to form communes where they could themselves lay the ground rules by which they would live. The others gathered en masse in the name of music, art and love (not to mention drugs) as together they dreamed of forming a more harmonious society. Unfortunately, it didn't really work. The communes failed, the hippies got jobs, sarongs turned into suits, and a new group of dissatisfied youth quietly began rallying not only against mainstream society, but against the newly shamed hippie subculture as well.

And then there were punks.

SUBCULTURE VS. SUBCULTURE

"The hippies wanted peace and love. We wanted Ferraris, blondes and switchblades."
—*Alice Cooper, musician*

When the idealism of the hippies proved to be little more than a pipe dream, a new generation of youth began questioning just what sort of lifestyle they now wanted for themselves. The mainstream culture remained firmly in the hands of the older generation, but the hippies' way of rebelling no longer held any appeal. If preaching love and peace didn't cut it, perhaps there was a better, more aggressive way. Where there were flowers and hugs, now there would be spikes and mosh-pits. Finding themselves distrustful of both the mainstream and the most pervasive subculture of the day, the punks set about creating their own personal version of identity and ethos. And if they couldn't draw their influences from their forebears, they would just have to create new ones for themselves.

> "What punk wrought was a Do It Yourself (DIY) attitude. Instead of sitting around worshiping the rock stars or gurus who supplied the people with dreams of one free ride or another, punk fans were encouraged to pick up their own guitar, or a mimeograph machine, or some old clothes— whatever was around and cheap—and express themselves."
>
> —*R. U. Sirius and Dan Joy, countercultural pundits*[19]

The punk movement blurred the line between producer and consumer, particularly when it came to music. Where hippies had gathered at massive festivals to see famous musicians perform, punks got together at small local venues to watch their own friends throw down. A sense of personal experimentation accompanied the punk philosophy, making it the most personalized subculture to date. This was not a group of people rallying against a common mainstream enemy (although that's not to say that they weren't anti-establishment). The punks were rallying against *everything* they'd seen so far. The hippie subculture had failed and the new punk subculture was the first to be born not just as subculture vs. mainstream, but as subculture vs. subculture. Rather than getting everybody together for a common cause, punk allowed youths to experiment with their own personal cause. As producers of the very culture they were now consuming, everyday kids were able to create the life they wanted to live and to express themselves the way they wanted to express themselves, ad hoc and on request. It was about being who you wanted to be and doing what you wanted to do, all on your own terms.

Once the punk mindset was born, it paved the way for the next wave of subcultures that would follow: the goths, the metalheads, the geeks, the ravers, and so on and so forth. If the first big subcultures were anti-mainstream and the next big subculture was anti-subculture, all of the subcultures that followed could be about finding like-minded people with similar ideas that they wanted to pursue, as opposed to finding other people who were against the same things you were against. It allowed groups to form as a positive—we are this, we believe in this—instead of as a negative—we are not that, we do not believe in that. The next step in our subcultural evolution was clear: narrow down the focus of each subculture to best suit the group of people involved. It was time to divide and conquer.

PUNK IS DEAD.
LONG LIVE PUNK.

WHEN THE FBI CAUGHT WHIFF of a young man threatening to bomb all of the trains in New York City, they quickly sprung into action. The man in question had written a letter expressing his frustration over the Transit Authority's war on graffiti and his bomb threat led the FBI to contact other graffiti writers, begging them to talk him out of it. The problem was, the threat never had anything to do with explosives. This guy was no terrorist-to-be, as any member of the graffiti subculture can tell you. He was a *writer*—a graffiti tagger—and *bombing* was just slang for spray-painting his tag onto the side of trains.[20] Fast forward a couple of decades and a whole new type of bombing has crept into the urban landscape—only instead of spray paint, this one involves a skill set traditionally reserved for grandmas and suburban housewives.

The yarn bombing movement launched in 2005 when a woman named Magda Sayeg decided to cover the doorknob to her Houston boutique in a custom-knit yarn cozy.[21] The resulting colorful intrusion into the asphalt gray of its metropolitan surroundings was an instant hit. Over the next few years, the movement would pick up steam, developing followings in big cities across the world, and guerrilla knitting would come into its own as a legitimate subculture.

"It's like graffiti with grandma sweaters."

—*Jessie Hemmons, yarn bomber*[22]

In a way, things had come full circle from the day of the flappers. Whereas the flapper subculture had allowed women to buy ready-made clothing without needing to create it themselves, nearly a century later, young women (and a few young men) would pick up traditional clothes-making handicrafts to use as their own customizable form of rebellion. The difference was that this time, instead of being obligated to make their own clothing, the new generation used their newfound skill to leisurely express themselves while bringing some color to the drab city streets. As one yarn bomber put it, "the expectation is that knitting has to be linked to something useful;"[23] by contrast, urban yarn bombing is purely aesthetic and has no tangible function. So although a new group of young women was now engaging in the same type of activity that their great-grandmothers had engaged in some hundred years earlier, there was one very major difference: now, they were doing it by choice and for their own personal reasons. This was not a subculture based on rebellion against societal norms. This was a subculture based on people doing what they wanted to do, and finding others who wanted to do the same.

ALL THAT SHE WANTS

Let's go back in time, to an era before the bombers and the punks and the hippies and the flappers. Let's go back to a time when your identity wasn't really up to you. For most of human history, who you were had to do with where you were born, who your parents were and what they did for a living. There were no big subcultures back then because (1) people were too busy trying to stay alive and well to even think about rebelling against their class and/or living situation and (2) it was nearly impossible to change the concept of who you were anyhow. Identity was something you were born into, not something you created on the fly from an a la carte menu of cultural choices.

> "Choice has replaced obligation as the basis for self-definition."
> —*James E. Côté and Charles G. Levine, sociologists*[24]

Consider that by the time the printing press was created, human beings had already been stomping their way across our fair planet for several millennia. Now consider that it took *centuries* after the invention of the printing press for even just the bible to hit an affordable level of widespread distribution. It would be decades more before any sort of cultural texts made their way into local teahouses and pubs, and still decades more before anything *sub*cultural could be legally printed and distributed. Information travelled at the speed of a human or a horse, and there was no real way to speed up the spread of ideas beyond that. Without the ability to share ideas across different geographical regions, subcultures based on shared views and aesthetics could only ever develop locally. And since subcultural ideas were traditionally practiced by very small percentages of the population, the only place they could *really* develop was in cities, where there were enough people around that those small percentages could actually find one another. That's why it's no mistake that America's first big subculture, the flappers, was born at the moment when more Americans started living in cities than in rural areas and the rise of the automobile allowed ideas to spread faster than ever before. For the first time in history, the tides had changed.

Once upon a more recent time—we'll call it the early 1990s—my mom took a trip to visit our relatives in Russia. She came back with a suitcase full of the usual assortment of homemade breads and jams from my grandmother and aunt, but also with something unexpected: an Ace of Base cassette that she just couldn't stop talking about. This was the latest and greatest thing, according to my mom, and *just wait* until I heard it. Well I did, and at the time I have to say I thought it was pretty darned cool (give me a break, I was a kid). Over the next couple of months, the tape grew worn and I had the lyrics fully memorized by the time their first big single hit American radio. It had taken time for the Swedish export to make its way across the ocean; the album had hit nearby Russia several weeks before it made its way onto the top 40 charts in the US. The timelines for the spread of a trend had gone down significantly from the days of the printing press, but it wasn't until the internet came along that the time lag disappeared altogether and we Americans could experience Swedish pop music at the same time as the Swedes (or the nearby Russians). It was the internet that brought the subcultural strength of cities—in other words, having so many people around that *some* of them are bound to be into the same things that you're into—out of physical space and into the virtual, where it could be accessed and spread by anybody, immediately. For better or for worse, Ace of Base could now hit the whole globe at once.

THRASH, SPEED AND DOOM

As the amount of personal choices has expanded relentlessly and the mainstream has shattered "into a zillion different cultural shards,"[25] people have begun pursuing their interests not as a matter of rebellion, but as a matter of course.[26] Technology has eliminated the time lag between the creation of a subcultural trend and its spread to the world-at-large, making "deviation from the norm [seem], well, normal."[27] The amount of possible choices has ballooned, and ballooned again, and ballooned once more, up to the point where people now classify themselves into smaller and smaller niches of society.

Let's take the metalheads for instance. Now I happen to be an obsessive music collector and a heavy user of internet service Last.fm, which keeps track of my musical preferences and allows me to join groups based on shared musical interests. Upon joining a couple of groups designated for people with particularly wide tastes in music, I couldn't help but notice that there was a whole lot of metal popping up within these supposedly diverse groups. Well it turns out that metalheads no longer cluster themselves under the single monolithic tag of "metal" (it also turns out that metalheads like creating these kinds of groups on Last.fm). Where there was once just "metal," now there is thrash metal, speed metal, doom metal, hair metal, power metal, avant-garde metal, Christian metal, death metal, Viking metal, and many more commas worth of unique metal subgenres. It also turns out that the hair metal listeners and the speed metal listeners don't really have mutual interests, nor do the nu metal listeners and the black metal listeners have many bands in common. These days, instead of having to align themselves with one big, catch-all version of their subculture, the metalheads have fragmented into many smaller, more specific subgroups that allow them to choose *exactly* which type of metal they like. This was no longer a question of creating a single subculture, much less one that rebels against a big societal "mainstream." What the metalheads have created is what the rest of society has lately been creating across all realms of life—they've divided themselves up into neatly dedicated *micro*cultures that specify *exactly* what they like.

(A brief technical note: sociologists have lately been moving away from the term "subculture," a field of study traditionally focused on deviant behavior, and are now more likely to use terms like post-subculture, neo-tribe or, my term of choice and one I will continue to use throughout this book, microculture.)

On the other side of the microcultural coin is the revelation that all of us are now, in some way or another, minorities. The ability to divide ourselves into smaller and smaller sections of society has spread us out so thinly that culture is no longer anchored by a single generic "mainstream," but is instead composed of hundreds upon hundreds of specifically targeted groups and microcultures. Although some of your interests are bound to be rather generic (I like sponge cake), others are just as bound to be highly specific (I like Japanese mochi stuffed with red bean paste). The growing availability of options across all spheres of life has given us the ability to experiment with more possibilities than were ever previously available. My parents never experienced the glutinous joy that is biting into mochi not because they were uninterested, but because it simply wasn't an available option (all the more so because they only immigrated to the US in the mid-70s). Having more possibilities available allows us to more specifically tune into *exactly* what we want, while also allowing us to tune out what we definitely *don't* want. And because the microcultures are more focused than the previously popular one-size-fits-all subcultures, you can be a doom-metal-listening, mochi-eating yarn bomber, and be able to simultaneously exist across several microcultures dedicated to each of your specific interests. Of course, you're bound to be a minority in many ways, but this new version of minority is one designated by choice, not by circumstance. Being a member of multiple minorities in this sense actually has its advantages—as sociologist Peggy Thoits points out: "Generally, the more role-identities individuals hold, the more purpose, meaning, behavioral guidance and approving social feedback they have available, and thus, the better should be their mental health or general well-being."[28]

TRASH, STEAM AND COSTUMES

At first glance, some of today's microcultures seem outright insane. Take cosplay for instance (short for "costume play"), a group of individuals dedicated to dressing up in elaborate costumes that represent a specific character from a movie, video game, comic book or animation. Or take steampunk, the subgenre of science fiction focused on combining a Victorian-era aesthetic with modern technology to create a fantastic realm that never actually existed. If dressing up isn't your thing, there's always the freegans, a collective of anti-consumerist urbanites that believe in sharing, recycling and—on the grosser side of things—dumpster-diving. Or if you're really into shock value, take a look at the furries, or any of the other fetishist genres of sexuality that have popped into existence as the internet has made pornography available in every shape, size, species and skill set.

The point here is not that some people have strange interests. The point is that people are now able to choose from a wider variety of interests—including the strange ones—and to freely experiment with highly targeted microcultures to see where their own alliances lie. I myself have DJ'ed at a steampunk party and have eaten dumpster-dived food, each of which opened my eyes to new elements of the world while ultimately making me realize that I wasn't particularly keen on joining either group. Having spent most of the last year living in the mountains of Colorado, I can also tell you that the hippie subculture is still alive and well, and all the more distilled for having survived in its current form—as a narrowly focused microculture instead of a widespread subculture. The same goes with the punks, as an afternoon in New York City's Tompkins Square Park will quickly reveal. Even though more and more microcultures continue to come into existence, the old ones aren't going away; they're just getting more concentrated. Hippies are more hippie. Punks are more punk. Health nuts take more vitamins and supplements. Food nuts eat more deep-fried Twinkies and KFC Double Down sandwiches. People have been given more options as to which particular microcultures they want to align themselves with and the micro-cultures themselves have grown increasingly focused and polarized. And as my own experiences with steampunk and freeganism demonstrated, it's easy to dip your toe into a new microculture without having to become fully involved. Not only do we have more options on all ends of the spectrum; we're now freer to experiment with them at our own pace.

Another key benefit of having more options is that we've become more accepting of different modes of self-expression. Mohawks were once a confrontational symbol of an anti-mainstream subculture. Now, my 2-year-old nephew wears one. It's a fair bet that in another ten or twenty years, modes of self-expression that seem outrageous now will become commonplace. It's a simple matter of cultural evolution, and the spread of multiple sub- and microcultures has been like a snowball rolling down a mountain. The flappers rebelled by showing their knees, the hippies rebelled by growing their hair, the punks rebelled by tearing their clothes, and as more and more groups joined in on the game, rebellion became less of a reason for our appearance than plain old self-expression. Though it may seem trite at first, we often dress the way we want to for no other reason than the personal amusement it gives us. What's not trite is that the ability to do so took many centuries of slow cultural development. In that sense, the rebellion of all the previous subcultures worked; they've made it socially acceptable to choose the exact type of life you want to live and the exact way you want to express your own personally constructed identity. Just ask any hipster.

THE RISE OF THE HIPSTER, THE FALL OF THE REBEL

YOU'D BE FORGIVEN FOR THINKING he was some kind of an alien or inter-dimensional being, or at the very least a lunatic escaped from some nearby asylum. Whether his face was covered in painted polka dots or a 360-degree wig that enveloped his entire head, when Leigh Bowery walked into the room, your eyes could be on nothing else.

> "Rather than, say, do a painting with canvas or sculpting with clay, I put all these ideas onto myself."
>
> —*Leigh Bowery, performance artist*[29]

It was the late 80s and early 90s, and Leigh Bowery was a startling example of a newly developed microculture called the club kids. This was a group of people wholly dedicated to having fun and nothing but fun. Their costumes were outrageously elaborate, elevating the simple act of self-expression to performance art and shocking the sensibilities of casual passersby. The clubs loved them because they brought in a crowd. The crowd loved them for being such a bizarre spectacle. And they loved themselves because they had found a way to make their living from just being themselves and having a good time.

As Leigh Bowery was making waves at the coolest and craziest clubs in London, a group of enterprising individuals headed by Michael Alig was partying it up on the other side of the ocean. At the height of their popularity, the New York club kids appeared on several daytime talk shows, defending their wild appearance to the shocked audiences and extolling the values of judgment-free self-expression. While a few core members of the scene went on to achieve success in the fashion industry, for most the partying lifestyle came to an abrupt ending when Michael Alig murdered his drug dealer and the club kids lost their figurehead and their hold on the New York clubs. But despite its dramatic ending, the club kids' message had been sent loud and clear: we will dress however we want to dress, and we refuse to accept your judgment.

MAINSTREAM INK

What Leigh Bowery and Michael Alig figured out is the same thing that some of the wilder hipsters have lately figured out: shocking people ain't what it used to be. The more cultural options have appeared on the scene over the past several decades, the more accepting we've (slowly) become of them. Mohawks, piercings, tattoos, dreadlocks—each used to be enough to incite scandal. So what exactly happened to change all that?

"Show me a man with a tattoo and I'll show you a
man with an interesting past."

—*Jack London*

Traditionally used as cultural symbols or markers of status dating all the way back to 3200 BC,[30] tattoos were more recently relegated to sailors, criminals, circus performers and other marginalized members of society. They carried some seriously dangerous overtones. Having a visible tattoo was a severe obstacle when it came to getting a job and the mere mention of one was enough to shock grannies and aunties everywhere. By the time the 1980s rolled around, tattoos had earned themselves a new adjective: *cool*. The arrival of MTV brought images of tattooed rock stars into the average American home and all across the country rebellious teenagers eagerly awaited their 18th birthday so they could legally join their ranks. Nowadays, multiple reality shows—including one on TLC, formerly known as The *Learning* Channel—prominently feature tattoo parlors and their patrons. According to a Harris poll conducted in 2008, more than 1 in 3 Americans aged 25-29 now has a tattoo.[31] (For the record, I am 30 and have three.) Tattoo artists and enthusiasts have lately been getting inked on the conventionally off-limits face, neck and hands in an attempt to demonstrate their dedication to the tattooing microculture, and even traditionally conservative Republicans are getting in on the game; one estimate has it that there are 7 million tattooed Republicans walking around the US.[32] Tattooing has gone mainstream and as with any legitimized trend, it all began with a small group of dedicated individuals.

Big fashion trends tend to start with those known as the early adopters. These are the cool kids, the innovators, the ones who decide yes, I want to do that, and I don't care who knows it. Early adopters are committed to making a statement, whatever their reason, and are willing to take the risk of being socially shunned in order to adopt something they believe in, such as getting a tattoo. The early adopters then begin spreading the idea to the second adopters, who may not have the same level of commitment as the early adopters but who admire their ideas or join in as an act of solidarity. The idea spreads further, to the third and fourth and fifth adopters. With each new group of people willing to join in, the idea gets a bit more diluted and a bit more acceptable. By the time parent-approved tween heartthrob Justin Bieber can non-controversially sport a tattoo, the style has been propelled into mass awareness and has lost the original associations given to it by the early adopters. And so it went with piercings, dreadlocks and mohawks, each taking on a different meaning by the time it was legitimized in mass culture. The line between being a rebel and being a conformist has grown hopelessly thin as traditional means of rebellion have hit mass markets and early adopters have had to go further and further into obscure fashions in search of something new. Enter the hipster, stage right.

AUTHENTICALLY COOL

Cool has always been a moving target. Once spotted, it moves further into obscurity, into the realm of the James Deans and the Jimi Hendrixes of the world. For most of us, by the time we hear that something is cool, there's a whole other group of people telling us that no, that thing is no longer cool, it's too well known to be cool. Cool is exclusive and it's elusive, but that doesn't stop us from trying to find it. There's even a whole new industry that's sprung out of trying: coolhunting. But what does it really mean to be cool?

A big part of being cool is unquestionably about your attitude, but there's more to it than that. It's about constantly chasing that moving target, adapting and moving on once your own personal trends start getting picked up by others. It's about the thrill of the chase, about constantly trying to find the newest, best thing out there and aligning with it for just long enough that others notice and acknowledge you for it, because let's be honest—being cool often means being noticed. The attitude has to be one of supreme confidence, no matter how absurd the style or the object. But the *really* cool people out there are the ones who are indifferent to your judgment, as the club kids once were. They are the ones who will wear what they want to wear and do what they want to do for reasons that are 100% their own. In that sense, having one of your personal styles make its way into popular fashion can be a real disappointment. As trends move from the early adopters to the late majority, they lose their original meaning. If you helped create that original meaning, it's a disappointment when it's lost. Then again, being cool means it's easy for you to move on because, once again, cool is a moving target. And so, for that matter, is authenticity.

A lot of the common complaints about modern hipsters have to do with their authenticity. It's said that they move far too quickly from trend to trend, living purely off of style without any substance. They're said to be inauthentic because they don't stick with anything long enough to develop beliefs around it. But who ever said that modern, choice-based identities are supposed to be static?

In the days when you were born into your identity and had little choice in rebelling against the matter, nobody could ever question your authenticity. You were who you were because you were born into it, and that was that. Now that we have the freedom to choose our identities and our alliances for ourselves, your motives can constantly be called into question. There is a need to justify who you are because it's assumed that who you are is who you *chose* to be. Modern society seems to be on a constant quest for authenticity; for being true to ourselves; for following our hearts; for being who we want to be. The unspoken message is that our personal identities are something to be discovered and that, once they are, we're meant to cling to them and hold them up as being our true, authentic selves.

Hogwash.

The concept of finding an authentic self implies that who we are is static and unchanging. It implies that we have some sort of core personality that we need to discover and be true to, but the days of static beliefs and unchanging culture are long since over. The timeline for the spread of trends has practically disappeared and the amount of cultural options we have been exposed to has grown relentlessly. We are constantly being presented with new options and constantly being questioned for the options we've already chosen. Believing that it's possible to find your authentic self is a bit like believing that it's possible to find what's authentically cool—what works right now might not be what works next year, or next month, or even next week. Being true to ourselves really means doing things that we enjoy and, while some of our interests and personality traits are bound to stay the same over time—just as leather jackets will always have their place in the annals of cool—some things are just bound to keep changing. In the words of musician Aimee Mann, "You're only as cool as your last project."[33] And so it goes with authenticity.

MR. BRO

"What's 'dude?' Is that like 'dude ranch?'"
"Dude means nice guy. Dude means a regular sort of person."

—*Easy Rider, 1969* [34]

"Let me explain something to you. Um, I am not 'Mr. Lebowski.' You're Mr. Lebowski. I'm the Dude. So that's what you call me. You know, that or, uh, His Dudeness, or uh, Duder, or El Duderino if you're not into the whole brevity thing."

—*The Big Lebowski, 1998* [35]

When Captain America got onto his motorcycle and rode off into the sunset in the 1969 film *Easy Rider*, he was off to pursue the dream of a life worth living, one outside of the mainstream and decided upon by his own terms. Similarly, when The Dude ditched all responsibilities to go bowling in 1998's *The Big Lebowski*, he was following the unspoken rule of cool: do what you want to do and don't worry about what other people think. Each film was pivotal for its generation, defining a cool aesthetic and providing a hero who lived life on his own terms and did his own thing despite any naysaying. But in the three decades that had elapsed between the two films, a lot had changed. In *Easy Rider*, our heroes meet a tragic ending as a result of their subcultural lifestyle. Much of the film is spent defending themselves against regular folks who just don't get why they have long hair and ride motorcycles. They are seen as a menace to be avoided. Although *The Big Lebowski* took a decidedly funnier approach to the subcultural David vs. mainstream Goliath story, the message was largely the same: the lead character was a rebel trying to live his life outside of the confines of day-to-day society. Only this time around, The Dude ran into conflict because of a random coincidence, not because he was shunned by everybody around him for his appearance.

Life in the 21st century is casual in a way that life in the 1960s never was, particularly in the United States. Back then, you wore a suit not only to go to work, but to go to a restaurant, to go to a theater, to get on a plane, or to do just about anything else that required leaving the house. You addressed your neighbors as Mr. and Mrs. Jones and they addressed you in the same way. Jeans were meant for farmers and physical laborers. You did not share the intimate details of your life with anybody but your nearest and dearest, and you definitely didn't share them anonymously or with strangers. Proper etiquette was vital and the fork always had to go on the left, even if you were eating one of those newly invented TV dinners. Rules were unspoken and social conventions dictated your actions depending on whatever situation you found yourself in. And you most certainly did not ask anybody to call you *Dude.*

Fast forward to present day and it doesn't take a Julia Child to tell you that everything has changed. Although many jobs still require you to wear a suit, increasing amounts of billionaires run their companies wearing jeans and a t-shirt. You are on an instant first-name basis with every telemarketer and store clerk you meet and would probably be considered stiff if you tried to introduce yourself to neighbors by last name only. Etiquette is reserved for fancy restaurants and business luncheons. We blog, we tweet, we update our statuses, and we share a remarkable level of detail about our lives with complete strangers. We speak in slang and we write in abbreviations. Having a nickname is cool and being able to go to work in your sweats is a sign of privilege, not slovenliness. The omnipresence of camera phones makes it easy to catch you off-guard and immediately share your image online with your friends, family and colleagues. Being formal is boring and stuffy. Being tactfully *in*formal is the new name of the game.

To be cool in previous eras meant to brazenly show off your informality. It was a sign of rebellion against societal norms and it took a lot of guts to so openly defy proper cultural conventions. These days, there's just not as much to defy. Even though social norms still exist and cause great amounts of judgment and gossip, people are no longer shocked as easily. Nonconformity becomes more and more difficult as conformity becomes more and more casual and has more and more iterations. Once, we sought to have freedom *from* doing what was required of us. Now, we want freedom *to* do what we want. The Captain America of *Easy Rider* would hardly be noticed today, nor would *The Big Lebowski*'s Dude turn many heads. In an age when we have every choice in the world constantly laid out before our eyes and can join as many microcultures as we want based on whatever our interests may be, we *do* have the freedom to do what we want. And even if we can't do it in person, we can always head over to the internet and do it all anonymously.

2 . . . . . . THE INTERNET
HAS CHANGED S

RULE 34

THAT'S IT. I'M UNSUBSCRIBING.

Such was the thought process of tens of thousands of people when movie rental service Netflix went through a prolonged PR disaster in late 2011. After first raising prices by 60% and then threatening to split off its DVD-by-mail service from its internet streaming service, scores of subscribers terminated or scaled back their accounts in protest of the unwelcome changes, myself among them. It wasn't until I was scrolling through a DVD kiosk's selection a few weeks later that I realized the error of my ways. Sure, I could still rent the newest Hollywood blockbuster, but where were my critically-acclaimed feel-good foreign movies? My mind-bending independent sci-fi & fantasy recommendations? My classic visually-striking cerebral films or my dark tortured-genius movies based on real life? The prices may have gone up, but it soon became clear that what Netflix provides is unparalleled in the offline world: an endless selection and outstandingly personalized curation.

As my brief time away from Netflix demonstrated, we've come a long way from the days of one-word movie genres like Drama and Comedy. It seems like every time you check, some new adjective has been added to the genre descriptions and the more Netflix you watch, the more specific your recommendations get, making you pause for a moment before realizing that yes, you really *do* like emotional mother-son movies with a strong female lead, and perhaps you'd have realized it earlier if Blockbuster had been wise enough to point you towards that particular aisle. Then again, no aisle that specific ever existed. In fact, there are a *ton* of things that never existed before the internet came unapologetically crashing into our day-to-day lives.

> "Rule 34: If it exists, there is porn of it."
> "Rule 35: If porn of it does not yet exist,
> it will soon."
> —*Generally accepted internet rules*
> *(original source unconfirmed)*[36]

In a way, the internet has ruined some things forever. It has shown me the Teenage Mutant Ninja Turtles doing things that the Teenage Mutant Ninja Turtles were simply never meant to do. I have seen Captains Kirk and Picard in ways I could never possibly have imagined them, and have come to cringe at seemingly innocent phrases like "lemon party" and "two girls one cup." These are all exemplars of Rule 34, generally thought to have been created on internet site 4chan to be invoked for various reasons on various message boards, most often by various teenagers. Rule 34 certainly represents one of the more lurid sides of the internet (and one you'll unfortunately run into whether you want to or not), but it was born for the same reasons that Netflix now provides 4- and 5-adjective genre descriptions: these days, there's just a whole lot more of *everything* around.

YOUR OWN
PERSONALLY CURATED CULTURE

In the year 2007 alone, the amount of digital content created, stored and replicated around the world added up to *3 million times* the amount of information in all of the books ever written.[37] By the year 2010 (and only in the year 2010), we produced 10 times the amount of data that we'd produced in 2007, getting us up to the point of 1.2 Zettabytes* and making me remember my elementary school days when a number like gajillion didn't seem quite so attainable. To get an idea of how much data that is, imagine enough paperwork to stretch from Earth to Pluto and back 16 times, or to cover every last square inch of the United States in paper three feet deep.[38] That's a whole lot of tweeting going on. And it's growing every year. No wonder it seems like there's a whole lot more information around these days—there is.

---

* 1 Zettabyte = 1 trillion gigabytes

CONTENT, CONTENT EVERYWHERE

The human brain can hold between

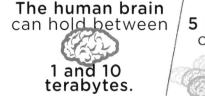

1 and 10 terabytes.

There are over **5 million terabytes** on **the internet.** [a]

EVERY MINUTE, ON THE INTERNET [b]

More than **168 million emails** are sent

Google serves nearly **6 million search queries**

Over 60 hours of video content are uploaded to YouTube

Approximately **82,000 status updates**, **135,000 photos** and **510,000 comments** are posted on Facebook

ONLINE VS. IN-STORE SELECTION [c]

MUSIC
iTunes
Walmart

MOVIES
Netflix
Blockbuster

BOOKS
Amazon
Borders

So what are we supposed to do with all of that constantly replenishing information? The answer is simpler than you might think: absolutely nothing. Your average internet user is never going to touch 90% of the information that's out there. There's simply too much of it and, when searching for a specific topic, any data not related to that topic—in other words, most of the data that's out there—is just background noise. The true strength of the internet—the one that's bringing about so many cultural advances and making us log back in all day, every day—goes back to the classic idea of the needle in the haystack. Knowing that a needle exists in the haystack is a fairly worthless piece of information. But knowing the *exact* location of the *exact* needle you're looking for at the *exact* moment when you need it—that's priceless. The unfiltered internet is about as useful as a room full of randomly torn-out encyclopedia entries. Sure, you might find something interesting, but it's not likely that you'll find anything relevant. It's not until that information is sorted, tagged, filtered and curated that it actually becomes valuable.

> "[Only] about 30% of what we rent is new releases…
> and it's not because we have a different subscriber.
> It's because…we help you find great movies that
> you'll really like. And we do it algorithmically, with
> recommendations and ratings."
> —*Reed Hastings, CEO, Netflix*[39]

When I open up my Netflix queue online, the hyper-specific genres laid out before me are custom-tailored based on my personal preferences. The strength of the service is not so much that it has 20,000 titles available to watch instantly; it's that it can show me the 1% of those titles that are most likely to appeal to me specifically. Instead of overwhelming us with the amount of data available, curation services like Netflix filter that data to transform the wholly impersonal into the exceedingly personal, and they perform the same process for every single user. Although a dozen of my friends may use the same service, it's unlikely that any two of us will see the same selection. By combining massive amounts of content with the ability to hyper-curate based on personal preferences, Netflix is just one example of what the internet has grown to provide: your very own personally curated culture.

Now that so much of the world's data is online, each of us has access to the same array of cultural building blocks. The internet has gathered the elements of our culture into a single, centralized, easily accessible virtual location. It has given us the tools to see not only the filtered, top 40 version of our culture, but also the raw data from which the top 40 was culled. It has given us the ability to see Casey Kasem's list and then turn around and create our own. With the help of curation services like Netflix, each of us can now personalize the elements of culture we access and interact with. We've arrived at a completely unprecedented point in human history—society still applies to us as a whole, but the way we actually *experience* culture is personalized. We may all play by society's *how*, but we each want to choose for ourselves the *what*.

MICRO MAJORITY

It's the 1960s. You're humming the latest Bobby Darin tune and heading over to the kitchen to get a cup of coffee when you run into Ted from Marketing.

"Did you see Walter Cronkite last night?"

"Sure did, Ted."

"Aren't those Beverly Hillbillies something else?"

"Sure are, Ted."

"Are you looking forward to Bonanza tonight?"

"Sure am, Ted."

Fast forward to present day. You've got that song from the new iPhone commercial stuck in your head and you're on your way to Starbucks for a Double Tall Extra-Hot Skim Mocha (no whip) when you run into Zadie from Sales.

"Oh hey, have you seen that new YouTube where the kids spill flour all over the house?"

"You mean the one with the food coloring?"

"No, no, that was last week, I mean the *new* one. I'll post it to your wall, it's great. Did you hear they're playing a John Waters retrospective at the indie theater this weekend?"

"Oh yeah?"

"Yep, I torrented a bunch of his films last week but I think I'll go check it out anyways. Here, lend me your thumb drive and I'll pass you a copy of *Serial Mom*."

Sharing cultural experiences with Ted in the 1960s was a given. As long as you both had TVs, odds were pretty good that you watched the same programming and listened to the same hits on the radio. Some 50 years later, it's not likely you've got much media in common with Zadie from Sales. Depending on your level of involvement with day-to-day internet aggregators such as Reddit and BuzzFeed, you may see *some* of the same content, but it's highly unlikely that your average media experience has much in common with that of your coworkers. In an internet-enabled culture, the hundreds of channels available on modern television are just the tip of the media iceberg. To share cultural experiences nowadays, you literally have to share the media you're experiencing, through direct file-sharing or by pointing others to the original source.

In the decades surrounding the 1960s, media was all about mega-hits. In 2012, we've entered the world of the micro: micro-hits, micro-blogging, micro-cultures, micro-celebrities, and so on and so forth. Now that the available amount of content has gotten so large, the size of a big hit has gotten correspondingly small. An old-school mega-hit took an audience of millions and was the apple of the pop culture's eye. A micro-hit isn't tied to any specific number; it's a cultural item popular within a given subset of people, far below the level of the country (or the world) as a whole. What's changed is the frame of reference, and it's the same reason that the prefix "micro-" continues to find new popular iterations. Although the principle behind being a hit within a small community is the same as it is within a large one and the *relative* size of the hit is the same, the *actual* size of the hit (or culture or celebrity) has greatly shrunk. Each hit reaches fewer people. Where there was one mega-hit, now there are a hundred micro-hits. And each and every one of them is custom-tailored to the community from which it emerged.

"[Brick-and-mortar] retailers will carry only content that can generate sufficient demand to earn its keep," *Wired* editor Chris Anderson argued in his 2004 book, *The Long Tail*. With only a limited local population available to generate that demand, retailers were left catering to the most popular items at the expense of relative obscurities. The new U2 album was guaranteed shelf space in your local music store; the debut album by that band you heard on college radio, not so much. It was Anderson who first described the rise of the micro-hit and the fundamental change in market size that gave rise to a new internet-enabled economic standard. "What the Internet presented," he wrote, "was a way to eliminate most of the physical barriers to unlimited selection."[40] In other words, it was the ability of the internet to reach beyond geographic boundaries and into markets based on interest that brought about the rise of the micro-hit. This isn't the global village once described by media theorist Marshall McLuhan.

This is the global storefront—and it's full of more options than McLuhan ever dreamed about. What's more, the internet's ability to provide personalized recommendations equips you with your own personal concierge. Enjoy that movie, did you? Here are a dozen more like it. Or, if you'd prefer, here's 4chan's dirty version of it, rule 34'd and ready to go. The choice is now entirely yours.

CHAPTER 2.2

1,000,000 STRONG
FOR ANYTHING

To the internet, it was just another case of spreading the word. To Amit Gupta, it was a problem with potentially fatal consequences.

When the 32-year-old web entrepreneur was diagnosed with acute leukemia in late 2011, he received some even more disheartening news: as an Indian-American, his odds of finding a badly needed bone marrow donor were only 1 in 20,000. A combination of an unusually small donor pool and an unusually high need for a close genetic match left Gupta with a single, all-important question: where could he go to find more donors?

A seasoned social media expert, Gupta immediately turned to his network of over 30,000 connections across popular sites including Facebook, Twitter and Tumblr to spread the word, organizing "swab parties" where potential donors swabbed the inside of their cheeks to obtain DNA. Despite encountering several dead ends and missing his initial 30-day deadline for finding a donor, good news arrived in late January 2012: Gupta had found a match and the transplant would proceed immediately.

Though at the time of this writing he is not out of the woods yet, his prognosis is greatly improved and Gupta's efforts have reportedly brought in 4,000 new donors. Moazzam Ali Khan, director of donor recruitment and community outreach at the South Asian Marrow Association of Recruiters and organizer of several donor drives on Gupta's behalf, describes the positive effects of the campaign: "These are now 4,000 [donors] who were not there before. That's 4,000 new hopes for South Asian patients."[41] Among them, Amit Gupta himself.

OTHERS LIKE US

"It's a small world after all. It's a small, small world."
—*Disney*[42]

The thing is, it really wasn't—at least not in 1964 when Walt Disney commissioned the Sherman Brothers to write that nagging earworm of a ditty to accompany his newly opened "It's a Small World" theme park ride.[43] The Iron Curtain was up, immigration rates were down,[44] and the internet was still but a twinkle in DARPA's* heavily protected eye. The ability of a single individual to inspire 700+ reposts in search of a genetic bone marrow match[45] was still many years ahead. Long before the online world became one big, border-free connect-a-thon, the offline world would experience some border-melding and culture-mixing of its own.

* Defense Advanced Research Projects Agency

OUR GLOBAL NEIGHBORS

PERCENTAGE OF FOREIGN-BORN AMERICANS a

PERCENTAGE OF AMERICANS WITH FOREIGN-BORN PARENTS b

1980 2007
39 Million 55 Million
Individuals speaking a language other than English at home, an increase of 140% from 1980. c

At the beginning of the last century, **1-in-8** U.S. residents was of a race other than white; at the end of the century, the ratio was **1-in-4**.
d

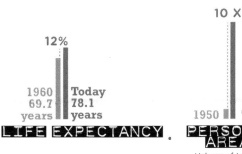

12%

1960 **Today**
69.7 **78.1**
years **years**

LIFE EXPECTANCY e

10 X

1950 **Today**

PERSONAL AREA f

Volume of territory through which one moves on a typical day.

30 X

1900 **Today**

RATE OF OVERSEAS TRAVEL g

Long before "google" was added to the Oxford Dictionary[46] and nearly half of all Americans opened up Facebook accounts,[47] incremental cultural changes were slowly pooling to make ours a small world, after all. Even neglecting the pervasive effects of the internet, we are living longer, traveling more and being exposed to more cultures and ethnicities than at any point in human history. Your average Joe is now exposed to more ways of living than ever before. Throw in the internet and Joe starts to notice a certain trend underlying the seemingly endless surge of diversity.

> "We are struck, as we use the internet, by the sense
> that there are others out there like us."
> —*Paul Hodkinson, sociologist* [48]

Take yarn bombing, for instance. Chances are pretty good that, unless you're a dedicated urbanite and/or street artist and/or heavy follower of modern trends, yarn bombing strikes you as a fairly obscure hobby. But do a search on Google and you'll see 937,000 pages that say otherwise. On Facebook, nearly 8,000 people like the Yarn Bombing page, and even Twitter returns a couple dozen results on a people search for the same. So what gives? Is yarn bombing actually mainstream?

Well, not quite. The popularity of yarn bombing goes back to the concept of the micro-hit. By no means is it a popular, mainstream activity, but the ability to find like-minded folks on the internet has allowed it to corral a following all its own. Yarn bombing isn't big. Football is big, with 376 million Google search results and 12.5 million likes on Facebook. Lady

Gaga is big, with 652 million search results and 46 million likes. But while yarn bombing may not be big, the existence of dedicated (not to mention current) Facebook pages, Twitter accounts and Tumblr blogs means anybody who's interested can easily join in on the fun, ad hoc and on request.

No matter how obscure your area of interest, these days the odds are pretty good that like-minded souls can be tracked down via the internet. Be they yarn bombing enthusiasts, nu metal head-bangers, steampunk aficionados or South Asian bone marrow donors, the internet has got them all—right down to your next-door neighbors.

ART FROM CRAIGSLIST

So a girl walks into a bar with a 6-foot-tall naked mannequin under her arm.

The punch line here is that this is no joke—I was that girl, the bar was in Astoria, Queens, the year was 2008, and I had just acquired the mannequin from a Free Stuff listing I'd found on Craigslist. The friend who was meant to assist me in getting the unwieldy thing home was running late and, it being a cold winter evening, I'd stepped into the most unassuming place I could find to lay low until my friend showed up to help me bring the thing home on the subway. The whole bar went understandably silent as I stumbled in through the front door with my awkwardly shaped free Craigslist prize in my arms. If you imagine that dream where you're in front of the classroom and naked, only now you're dressed and it's the 6-foot-tall mannequin under your arm that's naked (complete with insinuating crotch bulge), you'll understand about how I felt at that moment. After a quip about this being my ice-breaker that I carried with me all the time, the local crowd gladly welcomed me, albeit hesitant that this "friend" of mine was really on her way. At least, that is, until she showed up an hour later with an open slam of the door and a genuinely bewildered cry of, "Holy crap! That's just like the one I have at home!"

(For the record it really was, as a visit to her home proved a few months later.)

The often helpful, often leery, often just plain old bizarre world of Craigslist helps breach the divide between the online world and the real, physical one. On sites like Craigslist, online listings correspond to real-world items, jobs, housing and dates, bridging the gap between online and IRL,[†] and not without creating occasionally absurd scenarios such as the one in which I and my 6-foot-tall naked mannequin were the inadvertent stars. In the past, communication cost money, even when it was local. Placing an ad had a fee, even if you were just looking to give away a 6-foot-tall naked mannequin named Art. Posting goods, jobs, homes, vehicles—whatever you happened to be selling or seeking, you could be sure a price tag was attached. And that's assuming you could always find what you were looking for—or whom.

† Internet slang for "in real life"

Take online dating, for instance. Once considered the realm of the desperate and socially damaged, online dating has lately matured into a billion dollar industry,[49] with one in five singles having gone on a date with somebody they met through a dating site.[50] Dating services such as eHarmony and Match.com make use of the same kinds of recommendation engines that underlie services like Netflix and Pandora, connecting the personality dots and providing you with a shortlist of potential paramours. You may not have the guts to approach that pretty girl over in apartment 4C, but with the help of the internet now you can meet one on the other side of town who shares your passions for Doctor Who and geocaching. Mr. Right may not have come by the bar tonight to pick up your last Merlot, but you can always hop online and meet Mr. Potentially Right who will gladly meet up in person next week. Online dating doesn't replace real-world courtship rituals; it supplements them.

The initial lure of the internet often revolved around your ability to meet people on the other side of the world. The cool factor then was, "Hey wow, I'm talking to somebody in Iceland!" Now that the web has weaved its way into our everyday lives, we prize usefulness over novelty. The cool factor now is, "Hey wow, this guy lives right down the street!" And indeed, many of today's newest technologies are aimed at combining the internet with the real world, creating a hyperlocal, hypertargeted, interactive, augmented reality. Internet dating works because it combines personalized recommendations with the ability to access a far larger pool of people than you could possibly meet face-to-face. The same goes for online communities based around shared interests.

Before the internet, communities and subcultures formed only in cities large enough to allow certain types of individuals to find one another. Nowadays, the internet has become a virtual town commons accessible by all, allowing those communities to form online and eliminating the need to physically *be* in the city to participate. Even though our interests have become increasingly specific and the previously prevalent handful of subcultures has fragmented into thousands of unique micro-cultures, it's just as easy to find a dedicated cosplay group online as it is to find one dedicated to football. The ability to freely participate in these online communities means that even the most introverted and agoraphobic among us can join in on the cultural conversation, no matter how obscure their tastes and interests. The age-old human burden of loneliness becomes less of a problem when community is never more than a click away. The added ability to then participate in those communities in the real world, via increasingly popular meet-ups and location-based services, is changing the fundamental way we interact with our fellow man, woman and furry. After all, location is just another parameter in the search for like-minded souls. It doesn't matter whether you're looking for a bone marrow donor from across the world or a hot date from right across town—chances are, you can find a match online.

THE AGE OF THE REMIX

It's fun to find something cool on the internet.

It's even *more* fun to share it with somebody else.

Such is the ethos behind the wildly popular Reddit community, a social news website where eight million active users[51] submit content and vote it up or down in popularity and site ranking. With over 111,000 topical "subreddits"[52] and a voting-based comment system that encourages witty and relevant conversation, Reddit has drawn a fiercely devoted user base known for both its individual and group participation. The voting system that underlies Reddit encourages users to contribute their own comments and iterations of popular jokes and memes, rewarding those that make it to the top with thousands of views and a not insignificant amount of praise. The same system downvotes content that is facetious, disingenuous or malicious, keeping hooligans at bay and making it clear that such behavior will not be tolerated. Though individual participation is highly encouraged and rewarded, the Reddit community also has a keen sense of when it's time to band together as a group. Whether it's raising $70,000 over-night for a troubled orphanage in Kenya,[53] organizing a 40,000 participant-strong Secret Santa gift exchange[54] or just playing around with the Scumbag Steve meme,[55] the high level of user involvement spurred by Reddit has at its core a simple fact of human nature: it feels good to be in control.

ASK ME ANYTHING (AMA)

"Everything You Always Wanted to Know About Sex
(But Were Afraid to Ask)"
—*1969 book by Dr. David Reuben*

Now here's a novel concept for your modern, internet-connected Digital Native—once upon a not-so-long-ago time, racy and taboo knowledge was more than just a mouse-click away. There was, in fact, no easy way to find answers to those questions you were "afraid to ask," nor was there an easy and safe way to discuss such questions with others. The answers to those questions, provided you could find them in the first place, came from tightly controlled official sources, usually in the form of books, newspapers, TV and radio broadcasts. Though the then-prevalent hippie subculture encouraged you to question everything, it was vague when it came to how you could actually go about doing so. Therein lay a twofold com-munication conundrum of the pre-internet era: (1) how could you find answers to questions that were too taboo to ask? and (2) how could you be sure that the official story about anything was true when all you could access *was* the official story?

"IAmA guy that hasn't pooped in the month of August yet. Ask me anything about my extreme constipation."[56]
—*Reddit, August 2011*

"I am national correspondent for the Atlantic (and long-ago speechwriter for long-ago president Jimmy Carter) AMA"[57]
—*Reddit, February 2012*

From the curiously gross to the politically relevant and with a little bit of everything in between, the popular "Ask Me Anything (AMA)" subreddit is just one example of the kind of internet-fomented forum that breaks down the pre-internet barriers to communication and knowledge. Those previously unanswerable taboo questions can now be addressed not only through the static pages created on the early internet, but also through the active conversations fostered through the increasingly interactive modern internet. The ability to participate in such conversations anonymously means that being "afraid to ask" is pretty much a thing of the past.

More relevant to our cultural evolution is the modern ability to question the official story of companies, governments, teachers, parents and other authority figures. That old symbolic phrase touted by many a hippie—"Question Authority"—has now become a physical reality in the open world of internet communication and research. We are no longer willing to take big media news stories at face value, preferring instead to hop online and reference multiple sources to get the *whole* story, warts and all. We discuss them on social networks, share feedback on blogs, and generally do our best to get involved with the stories that interest us (now that it's actually possible to do so). And at a time when the deaths of Osama Bin Laden and Whitney Houston are hitting Twitter and Facebook before they're hitting CNN and Reuters, the purveyors of the official story are no longer able to hide like the wizard behind the curtain. The ability to communicate freely online has empowered us as a society in a way that is, as with so many cultural trends spawned by the internet, a first in human history. Not only can we now find out the whole truth and everything but the truth; we can actively participate to change official policies for the better.

Take the Stop Online Piracy Act (SOPA), for instance. Boy, did the internet hate that one. As news of the freedom-curtailing act made its way from Facebook friend to Facebook friend, many of us bounded together to spread knowledge, sign petitions, contact politicians, and finally to participate in an unprecedented blackout that stretched to some of the most popular sites on the internet (Reddit and Wikipedia included). The day before the blackout, SOPA had only 31 opponents in Congress. The day after, that number more than tripled to 101.[58] Two days after that, SOPA was declared dead in the water and the battle was already over. While many declared that the internet had won out, in reality the truth stretched deeper than that. It was we the people who had won, and it was the ability to freely communicate online that had tipped the scales of justice in our direction. Perhaps Time Magazine put it best when it declared *you* its 2006 person of the year:

"The new Web... is a tool for bringing together the small contributions of millions of people and making them matter."[59] Underlying that fact: freedom of communication.

READ ONLY --> READ/WRITE

"No mommy, let *me* do it."

Perhaps no phrase is as indicative of the fundamental need for control that seems to be hardwired in the human brain[60] as is this common childhood utterance. Our first experiences with control take the form of actions without a framework—touching things, grabbing them, shaking them, kicking them. As our minds mature and we gain control of our motor functions, our actions become more complex. We put the round peg in the round hole and stack the small ring over the big one. By the time we toddle our way up into childhood, simple movements transform into structured play and games. We quickly learn that while moving things around aimlessly might be interesting, taking the time to learn the rules is what really makes a game fun. To learn we must first observe, temporarily relinquishing our control in the process. Once we've understood the rules, we gain a whole new level of control and suddenly Hungry Hungry Hippos becomes more than just a collection of things to shove up your nose. Is it any great surprise then that, after taking some time to observe and learn the framework and rules of the internet, we're ready to regain the control that comes so naturally to us?

"Today's audience isn't listening at all—it's participating."
—*William Gibson, science fiction writer*[61]

Ours has become a world of mashups, a world of memes, a world of remixes and fan fiction and ubiquitous blogs and Tumblr reposts, all of which allow users to create something new within the framework of something that already exists. While our first online experiences involve observation—learning the rules of the game, watching how others play, thinking about what we would do if it was our turn—the fun doesn't really start until we join in and start playing for ourselves. We get our feet wet by joining user-friendly social networks, posting simple content like status updates and photos and commenting on other users' posts. On a site like Reddit, most people start as lurkers, observing but not participating, before finally feeling comfortable enough to join in on the conversation. Once we've dabbled in adding our own content online, we get more brazen. We leave more comments on more sites, post videos as well as photos, and start reposting the content we find in our daily observations. The more we participate, the more others participate with us, drawing us further in and making us search for still newer ways to contribute—and there are plenty of companies out there lining up to help us do just that.

As more and more internet and software companies hit the market, we're provided with more and more ways to interact with content, and that interaction is getting easier with every passing year. Most computers now come pre-loaded with basic music-, photo- and video-editing software, giving everyday users access to tools that cost thousands of dollars just a couple decades ago, and tens of thousands a couple decades before that. Combine the availability of production tools with the ease of posting and sharing content online and it's no wonder that there are literally *billions* of posts, videos, photos and status updates added to the internet each and every day. And now that those production tools are making their way into our mobile devices as well as our home computers, those figures are only likely to increase.

The upshot of all this new content we're adding is an explosion of productivity, innovation and self-expression. Sure, there may be hundreds of silly new meme photos added to sites like Reddit on a daily basis, but there's also that one guy who decided a new tool was needed to house those photos and created Imgur, a site that now attracts 16 trillion views a month.[62] And yes, though most of the 60 hours of video added to YouTube each and every minute is bound to be junk, it's also the site that gave birth to the Justin Bieber phenomenon and arguably gave tween girls one of the more wholesome role models it has seen in some time. Hearing those success stories gives your average internet user all the more reason to chip in her own talents, and even if they never do reach beyond her own circle of friends, the ability to freely express herself and receive positive feedback from those close to her will have made the experience worth it anyhow.

The internet has thus fueled a shift from what media theorist Laurence Lessig called a Read Only culture into what he calls a

Read/Write culture. It is a version of culture that encourages more than just the passive consumption indicative of classic media including books, television and music. With the tools of production increasingly at hand, we're free to throw our own contributions into the pot, ad hoc and at will (like this self-published book, for instance). Whether we're creating something from scratch or altering pre-existing content, most of us now have the tools to produce and publish readily awaiting at our fingertips, and they're pretty much free to boot.

Just as a kid might initially enjoy watching his older brother play video games, we know the real fun doesn't start until we have the controller in our own hands—which, culturally speaking, we already do. And just as that kid might then enjoy playing the same games his older brother did, he'll quickly realize that he'd much rather choose the games for himself. Playing copycat may be fun at first, but it's a bit like playing a game without knowing the rules in that it's really only half of the fun. It's not until we move beyond copycat and create something worth copying that the real fun begins. And once we do create that something, we've got an instant audience ready to test it out on—our Facebook friends.*

* Or Twitter, or MySpace, or LinkedIn, or Pinterest, or Path...

3. . . . WE´VE CHANGED
OUR IDENTITIES

FACEBOOK MADE ME DO IT

FIRST HE BECAME A FAN OF MAYONNAISE. Then, money. Soon he was asking his friends for advice on a good place to get his chest waxed. He made flippant and increasingly distressing status updates, left irreverent and absurd comments on friends' posts, and finally confessed that, after not showering in several days, he had started to wonder: "Why bother?"

That was the point at which my friend Jason changed his password and cut off my control of his Facebook account. The year was 2009 and Jason and I had engaged in a little social experiment. He had wanted to see what would happen if he outsourced his Facebook account. Eternal joker that I am, I took it as an opportunity to wreak social havoc. I had full reign of Jason's Facebook profile for nearly two weeks before he cut me off. Admittedly, I'd been given a couple of warning calls first. The chest-waxing thing didn't go over too well, for instance, Jason being a straight man living in a largely gay New York neighborhood. But I persevered. The last straw was the status about not showering, something he hadn't even seen until going into work one day and being asked by not one but several colleagues, "So have you showered yet or what?"

The online experiment Jason and I perpetrated had some real-world social consequences. While I was playing a game, seeing just how far I could push it and finding endless amusement in Jason's exasperated accounts of finding out about his own status updates secondhand, Jason was receiving some very real feedback from his very real friends who'd seen his not-so-very-real updates. Though Facebook wasn't as big then as it is now, boasting a paltry 200 million users[63] to its current 845 million,[64] Jason's outsourced updates hardly fell on deaf ears. And with nobody expecting Jason's posts to come from anybody but Jason himself, all of my silly jokes were taken to be true. Without either of us realizing it until after the fact, what had really happened soon became obvious: I had temporarily tarnished Jason's identity.*

YOU VS. YOU VS. YOU

"This above all: to thine own self be true."
—*William Shakespeare*

Before we address the question of how the internet has fundamentally altered our identities, it's important to understand what identity means in the first place. At its simplest, identity is who you are. It is what makes you, *you* and me, *me*. It is the answer to the question, "Who am I?," and also the answer to, "Who do I think you are?" It is the definition of both the self—I am this, I am defined by this—and the other—you are

* Name changed to protect privacy

that, I define you as that. As such, each of us carries multiple identities, and we don't even have to be afflicted by schizophrenia or multiple personality disorder to do so. Your identity is not only who you think you are; it is also who I think you are. It is who your mom thinks you are, who your friends think you are, who your boss thinks you are, who your kids think you are. It is who you are when you're at work vs. who you are when you're at a party. It is the way you define yourself, the way others define you, and the way you are defined by a situation. It is up to you and it is up to others. In other words: identity is a much messier concept than we tend to give it credit for.

First up, there's you as you. This is you as you think you are, and without reference to anybody else. This is the you made up of your individual characteristics.[65] It is the you that you are representing every morning when you open up your closet and decide what to wear. It is the you in the mirror, and how you think about the you in the mirror. This *you* is the essence of your personal identity: it is you as you think of yourself.

When it comes to others, a different type of identity comes into play: you as others think you are. Now you might consider yourself a very pious individual, but if you're out there every weekend boozing it up and bringing home one-night stands, others aren't likely to see you as all that pious. Similarly, I happen to think I'm pretty funny, but if my humor doesn't strike a chord with you, "funny" will not constitute part of my identity to you. This second type of identity—you as others think of you —is therefore subject to personal judgment. Each of us defines both our own identity and the identity of others based on our personal worldviews. Now where we get those worldviews in the first place is a matter for another book entirely, but suffice it to say that each of us has a slightly different way of looking at the world around us. Therein lies a disconnect that is at the heart of so many social and personal problems: who I think I am does not always match who *you* think I am. And it gets more complicated still.

Our identities are meant to provide a sense of continuity over time and in various situations (indeed, the word identity comes from the Latin root *identitas*, meaning sameness). Identities provide a system for classifying the world around us, for knowing who is who and what is what without having to redefine the wheel every time we step out of the front door. When it comes to our social identities, the situations we find ourselves in define which parts of ourselves we choose to show. Though you may be one heck of a beer pong player, work is probably not the time to demonstrate that fact. You may love cursing and talking in slang, but you're likely to shift verbal gears before going to church. Although you may be the same *you* whether on vacation or in a meeting with a big client, the social rules surrounding your environment dictate which parts of yourself you're going to show.

Here's the good news: one of the best indicators of how happy we are is how comfortable we are with ourselves.[66] It's a no-brainer when you think about it: higher self-esteem = higher level of overall happiness. And one of the keys to high self-esteem is to align those different versions of *you*. If who I think you are jives with who you think you are, you don't have to spend any time worrying about how you'll be perceived and can feel comfortable just being yourself. It's the same reason that old friends are the best friends; they are the ones who know us inside and out and are OK with our foibles and eccentricities. So the question becomes simple: how do you align those different versions of your identity to create a cohesive whole?

THE SOCIAL ANIMAL

"Sex appeal is fifty percent what you've got and fifty percent what people think you've got."

—*Sophia Loren, actress*

Back in 1993, *The New Yorker* published a now-famous comic by Peter Steiner depicting two dogs in front of a computer. "On the internet," says the one at the keyboard, "nobody knows you're a dog." Fast forward two decades and the opposite has come true: not only does everybody know you're a dog, they know your breed, age, friends, habits and quite possibly where you went after obedience school last Tuesday night. The vast majority of us—65% of online adults[67] and 80% of online teens[68]—are now participating in social networking sites, with more people joining in every month. And with more than half of all Facebook users logging in every single day,[69] it's a fair bet that our participation is quite active. Our online identities have become far more than just a fad or a joke. They have become a part of who we are and how we define ourselves.

Perhaps then it makes sense that people reacted so strongly when my friend Jason outsourced his Facebook account to me. While we were having a laugh, Jason's Facebook friends were witnessing some very bizarre changes in their friend's behavior; after all, people tend to take Facebook pretty seriously when it comes to honesty. My updates to Jason's profile had caused a rift between who he really was and how his friends perceived him, one that was all the more pronounced because Jason was fairly unaware of the rift as it was going on. Once our experiment was over and he reclaimed his profile, Jason told his friends what had happened and the rift was closed. Who he really was and how he presented himself were once again in sync, and now his friends could joke about the absurdity of the experiment as opposed to the absurdity of not showering for days on end.

As we decide which portions of our identity to present online and how we're going to present them, what we're really deciding is how we want to be perceived by others. We do our best to portray ourselves in a way that is not only authentic, but also ideal.[70] What we reveal is up to us, and so we show only the best and most interesting parts of ourselves, hoping that our identities as perceived by others will match up with the best parts of our identities as perceived by us. When it comes down to it, we can't deny that we judge others, and so we know that they must be judging us. *What an awesome outfit. He looks terrible in that picture. Did she really go out with that guy?* Knowing that judging others is a fundamental part of our humanity, we attempt to present only that which can be judged positively. We want to look cool, interesting, fun, smart. *Here's a picture of me at a Kraftwerk show. Here I am surfing in Oahu. Just look at this photo of me reading Kafka.* With social networks humming 24/7 and everybody participating in the same social game, consistently showing the best parts of ourselves takes active work. Taking somebody else's experiences and passing them off as your own is a big internet no-no. And so we try to appear more interesting in the only way that works—by actively *becoming* more interesting. The part of our real-world identity we brought online thereby follows us back offline. So why do we do put so much pressure on ourselves to appear interesting? Simple: we don't want to be alone.

> "If a tree falls in the forest and no one notices its fundamental dopeness, it is not hip."
> —*John Leland, author of* Hip: The History[71]

It's long been known that human beings are social animals. Social isolation and loneliness have been proven to affect our health in a way comparable to high blood pressure, lack of exercise, obesity or smoking.[72] Brain scans show that the emotional region of the brain affected when we experience rejection is the same one that registers emotional response to physical pain.[73] The worst punishment you can receive in prison continues to be solitary confinement. To put it bluntly: being lonely sucks. And so we try not to be.

For the same reason that we're more likely to participate in games after learning the rules, we're more likely to be active within our social networks after we observe others being active on them. We see all the cool, interesting and fun things our friends are doing, and we want to do the same. It's been called FOMO, or "Fear of Missing Out," and its effect on human behavior comes from that same fear of loneliness we humans are so naturally endowed with. If all of your friends are out at a party on Saturday night, do you really want to be home alone with just that bag of Cheetos and the third season of 24? In the pre-social networking days, it didn't really matter since you wouldn't hear about the party until it was long over anyways. Nowadays, you get a play-by-play of the action scrolling through your ever-ticking news feed, heightening the fear of missing out and making you vow that next weekend, you'll leave Jack Bauer at home where he belongs.

Once you do join in on the fun and start participating more actively, those negative emotions turn positive. Instead of missing out, you're joining in. A recent study out of the University of Texas – Austin, shows that Facebook has a positive impact on our social lives, making us more sociable and providing opportunities for "new expressions of friendship, intimacy and community."[74] Another recent study out of Cornell University reveals that Facebook actually helps boost people's self-esteem.[75] Again, at the heart of all this data is a no-brainer: relating with friends good; being lonely bad. And so the online and offline expressions of our identities become codependent and next thing you know, that need to put our best face forward starts to creep into all aspects of our lives. Tit for tat.

I WANNA BE ADORNED

BEFORE THERE WERE IPHONES OR ANDROIDS or even a wireless internet, the roaming telecommunication device of choice was the beeper, also known as the pager. Propelled into popularity at a time when cell phones were too big and expensive to reach a wide audience, this simplistic device allowed others to call you and leave an alphanumeric message requesting a call back. Teenagers all across the US quickly developed a system of beeper communication based on numerical codes and then-popular hip hop group A Tribe Called Quest declared their "beeper's goin' off like Don Trump gets checks."[76] But with few technological innovations beyond "check screen, get message," manufacturers were soon left wondering how to sell users a new version of a device they already owned.

That's when Motorola decided to release a new beeper whose updated surface was more important than its upgraded innards. Banking on the idea that the then-ubiquitous black beeper had grown boring and predictable, Motorola decided to release a new device that was bright green. The result?

"All the fancy-ass technological engineering in the world couldn't get us a nickel more for the product," recounts a former Motorola pager executive, "but squirt-gun green plastic, which actually cost us nothing, could get us fifteen bucks extra per unit." It was a victory of form over function and a precursor to the cell phone cases, customizable laptop skins and multicolor kitchen appliances that are so popular today. The customers had spoken, and their message was clear: design matters.[77]

PIMP MY TOASTER

"People don't just buy products. They also buy a representation of themselves."
—*Chip Conley, CEO, Joie de Vivre Hospitality*[78]

As modern culture continues to stomp along and shake up everything in its path, it's comforting to know that some things stay the same. Like toasted bread, for instance. It has to be one of the simplest and oldest foods around, adapting to culinary changes while ultimately staying the same. It's one of the few foods that fits just as well alongside a classic meal like fried eggs as it does beneath a gourmet fusion like Sautéed Foie Gras sur Brioche. But before you get to the toast, you have to get the toaster, and that's when the sweeping changes of modernity are quick to catch up. Two slices or four? Stainless steel, black, white, red or another color altogether?

Numeric dial or digital display? Would you like a built-in egg poacher, perhaps, or an integrated mini-oven? Or maybe you'd just like the model that toasts a picture of Hello Kitty onto your bread. Whether you're looking for a $15 no-frills device or a $300 souped-up version created by Italian car designer Bugatti,[79] the simplest of breakfast foods quickly becomes anything but. It turns out the internet isn't the only part of modernity that's imbued with endless options.

Back in 1970, the average number of items available in a North American supermarket was 8,000.[80] These days, there are 38,000.[81] Starbucks alone boasts 87,000 possible drink combinations,[82] taking the classic "cream or sugar?" question to a whole new level. As for toasters, I found over 1,400 results listed on Amazon alongside nearly 200 types of bread, and let's not even get started on jam or jelly or marmalade. We're in the middle of an unprecedented variety boom and, though some decry the resulting "paradox of choice," it's hard to deny the joy of finding the *exact* type of doodad you were hoping to buy. Armed with little more than a credit card and a computer, the whole world of material goods can now be yours, and chances are even the shipping and handling are free.

Among the more important purchases we make nowadays are our devices, those various electronic whatsits and whatnots that fuel our modern lives and keep us plugged in whether at the desk, on the couch or in the car. What has traditionally been called personal technology, referring to the user's relationship with the device, has lately shifted to become personal*ized* technology.[83] Not only do you want the latest iPhone, you also want the coolest case, the most useful apps, the hottest new ringtone and the best accessories to outfit your new toy. Buying something unique off-the-shelf may be cool, but tricking it out to be *exactly* what you want makes it better than cool—it makes it yours.

Or take a look at cars, another important purchase that lies at the intersection of function and desire. In the 1960s, a single model of sedan—the Chevrolet Impala—accounted for over 1 in 8 car sales in a market made up of less than 40 types of cars. Nowadays, the car market is comprised of over 250 models, each with a wide array of options and extras, and fewer than 10 of which manage to grasp even 0.5% of the market.[84] When it comes to customization, even that's not enough, as a $3 billion car tuning industry[85] and dozens of international off-shoots of the car customization show "Pimp My Ride" easily attest. Paradox of choice? Maybe. But that doesn't mean we don't want the options.

TRANSLATE MY OUTFIT

"The only thing that separates us from the animals is
our ability to accessorize."
—*Steel Magnolias*[86]

Well, that and walk-in closets. After all, is there any better indication of the modern obsession with personal appearance than our need to have an entire *room* dedicated to housing our threads, kicks and baubles? There's clothes for work, clothes for working out, clothes for going out, clothes for staying in, clothes for fancy occasions, clothes for going to the beach, clothes, clothes everywhere. Different types of situations require different types of clothing, and at a time when pretty much everybody around you is carrying a camera-enabled smartphone in their pocket, your poorly chosen outfit could very well follow you long after the party is over and the last of the wine has been poured.

More than just a carrier of social norms, what we wear is an outward demonstration of who we are. Before you even utter the words, "Hi, my name is," your outfit has already sent a message. Clothing, in that sense, is not only a tool for covering ourselves up; it is a tool for communicating who we are. Wearing gold lamé to a funeral communicates just as loudly as showing up with a boombox blasting ABBA. Showing up to the office dressed in hot pants and a tube top does the same. It's *loud*. What we wear shows who we are and how we want to be perceived. No wonder The Container Store has become so popular; when clothing is communication, it's important to have a closet full of the right things to say.

Provided you're not living in a nudist colony, there's a certain set of daily rituals you use to prepare yourself before leaving the house—grooming, dressing, preening, pruning and otherwise priming yourself for public appearance.[87] Where you're planning on going dictates the social norms required for your outfit, but the rest is up to you. Do you want to fit in or stand out? Are you going for classic chic or a modern conversation-starter? Underlying these questions is a basic fact of identity:

how do I want to be perceived by others? Whether consciously addressed or not, how we dress is a way of telling people who we are and how they should think about us. But what happens when the signals get crossed and the meanings confused?

At a time when each of us is exposed to more cultural and personal options than ever before, misinterpretation of intent has become a common problem. I might think that this giraffe-print polyester vest shows that I'm open-minded and fun-loving, but to you it may appear childish and—dare I say it—*hipster*. Similarly, you might think those big diamond earrings you've got on show that you're classy and sophisticated, but to me they might just be plain old pretentious. Though each of us is now exposed to more ways of dressing, more modes of fashion and more types of personal style in a single day than our grandparents were in an entire decade, the norms governing those different iterations of self-expression have not yet been agreed upon. You may know how to judge which type of blazer is appropriate for a tenured professor, but assuming that you know how to judge a particular type of mustache that has just reentered the cultural zeitgeist after years of obscurity is far less certain.

Just a century ago, nobody owned more than a few basic outfits for a few basic situations. Their options were limited and the message sent by each outfit was obvious and widely understood. Now that our options have increased exponentially—and on-demand 3D-printing technology is on the horizon to increase those options further still—our clothing still talks, but we're all speaking different languages. This is not the conformist, jumpsuit-wearing future once imagined by *Star Trek* and *Logan's Run*. This is a full-on express-a-thon, only without the benefit of a Douglas Adams-inspired babel fish to translate what each of us is trying to say. We're confusing each other in the name of expressing ourselves. Thankfully, the confusion can be easily corrected. All we need to do is recognize that our wires are crossed. We've progressed too quickly, picking up too many stylistic iterations and losing their meanings along the way. Until we can all agree upon what exactly it means to wear a pair of Wayfarers, we ought to just lay off of the judgment and realize that what I think it means doesn't necessarily match what you think it means, and let's just agree not to even ask Auntie Mabel from Nantucket for her opinion quite yet. We're confused enough as it is.

MOTHER NATURE, FATHER INTERNET

"DOES GOD EXIST?"

This is my little brother, he is 7 years old, and my father is the one fielding this loaded question while tucking him into bed one night. My father, eternal pragmatist that he is, answers thusly:

"Well, nobody really knows for sure. Some people believe he does, some people believe he doesn't. Everybody has a slightly different opinion. It's hard to say."

My little brother is understandably confused by this answer. He lays back, furrowing his brow in thought, considering the question further, when suddenly his eyes open wide and his whole face lights up in a smile.

"I know, dad!" he exclaims. "Let's google it!"

PARENTS THESE DAYS

Ah, out of the mouths of babes. To adults raised at a time before the ubiquitous internet, my little brother's idea that the answer to a question as fundamentally spiritual as the existence of God is hopelessly silly. Of *course* Google can't give a definitive answer to a question based on belief. But to digital natives like my little brother, kids who learn how to use a mouse long before they learn how to tie their shoelaces,[88] the idea that they *can't* find an answer online is the silly one. Our version of curiosity involved mulling questions over and discussing them with friends. Their version is more easily satisfied: if you have a question, just look up the answer. Simple. Nor, despite our prevalent naysaying, can we honestly deny that we would've loved to have the internet around to answer our own questions when we were kids. Just as parents in the 1950s lamented the television and parents in the 1980s lamented the video game, nowadays parents of digital natives are lamenting their offspring's perpetual connection to the internet.

And they certainly are connected.

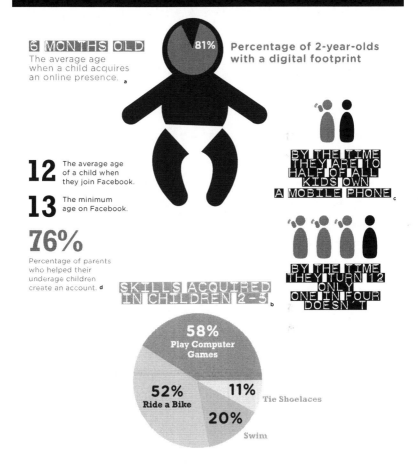

6 MONTHS OLD
The average age
when a child acquires
an online presence. a

81%

**Percentage of 2-year-olds
with a digital footprint**

12 The average age
of a child when
they join Facebook.

13 The minimum
age on Facebook.

76%
Percentage of parents
who helped their
underage children
create an account. d

BY THE TIME
THEY ARE 10
HALF OF ALL
KIDS OWN
A MOBILE PHONE c

BY THE TIME
THEY TURN 12
ONLY
ONE IN FOUR
DOESN'T

SKILLS ACQUIRED
IN CHILDREN 2-5 b

58%
**Play Computer
Games**

52%
Ride a Bike

11%
Tie Shoelaces

20%
Swim

As culturally zeitgeist as it is to decry the reliance of today's kids on technology, it turns out we adults are the ones who forced that reliance on them in the first place. The freedom that kids once had to run around outdoors has been severely diminished over the years,[89] with "go play outside" now more likely to refer to a fenced-in backyard than a park down the street. Even once they're considered old enough to leave the house unsupervised, teenagers run into problems in parks and malls where their presence is considered threatening and they're likely to be shooed away. So what's a kid to do if he can't go outside? Easy: go online.

Not only are today's kids likely to have their own bedroom all to themselves; that bedroom is likely to come fully equipped with a TV, computer and some sort of video gaming system. Even before they're armed with their own arsenal of portable and home technology, digital natives get their first exposure to the ever-connected modern world by watching their parents and siblings. There's that little white box that mommy's always staring at and talking to, that big black one that daddy un-folds and pushes buttons on while sitting at the table, those little white things with the buttons on them that big sis is always waving around, and a whole lot of other glowing squares about that do funny things when you slide your fingers on them. In 1997, the TV show *The Teletubbies* caused controversy as the first show to be targeted directly towards 1-year-olds.[90] Just over a decade later, nobody bats an eyelash at the dozens of apps geared towards babies and toddlers or the specialized furry cases used to convert tablet devices into interactive stuffed toys.[91] The norms have changed, the technology's gotten cheaper, and sitting little Suzie in a stroller with a pacifier and an iPad now seems like a perfectly normal thing to do.

With all that early exposure, most kids have been shown to develop an adult understanding of the technical complexity of the internet by the time they hit the sixth grade.[92] It's something that any parent of a digital native has noticed: when it comes to technology, it's the kids who are the real experts. And while parents are busy setting up filters to monitor and limit their kids' internet usage, studies show that those kids are having a blast trying to get around them.[93] We can lament it all we want, but the fact is that not only are the kids online, they're probably better at it than we are. And not only does the internet influence the way they *think;* it actively influences who they *become.*

MY PROFILE, MYSELF

In the spring of 2011, a good friend of mine invited me into his sixth grade Colorado classroom to talk with his students about identity, privacy and social networks. At the end of our sessions, I gave each class a survey to see just how many of them were already using sites like Facebook. My own findings confirmed those of other, larger studies. Of 65 surveyed students with an average age of 12, 63% admitted to using social networks. Of the ones on social networks, 56%

were using them once or more a day. When asked their favorite thing about social networks, they praised the ability to communicate with friends (even "over the summer," "if I'm sick" or "don't have my phone"), the ability to "express yourself in a different way than in person," "being able to post comments/ideas" and "putting my opinion out about things."

When it comes to figuring out who they are and how they want to express themselves, digital natives see little difference between the online self and the offline, physical self. These multiple representations form an overall identity,[94] one that carries through across different sites as easily as it does it across different outfits. Young people tend to use online technology to talk with people they already know and, for many, peer socialization, relationship-building and "hanging out" mainly takes place online.[95] Choosing not to participate in the social networks frequented by their peers can be socially disastrous, creating an unspoken obligation to join in or be left out completely. And with many friendships now being formed in the real world and solidified online, the process of getting to know each other better—in other words, sharing information about themselves to establish trust—is also taking place online.[96]

Beyond simple communication, digital natives have shown themselves to be highly creative, with 38% of teens sharing content they've created online and 26% remixing existing content.[97] As noted in the 2011 book *Dancing with Digital Natives: Staying in Step with the Generation That's Transforming the Way Business Is Done*, "In the natives' world, the tools of content creation... are free (or cheap) and readily accessible. And they have been that way since a native first thumbed his name into a smartphone... Natives find it exhilarating that they, themselves, are the editors, directors and actors in their own entertainment."[98] In the mind of the digital native, self-expression and content creation begin to merge, providing the lifelong ability to experiment with who they are and what they want to say. As for the rest of us, that socially accepted ability to experiment with your identity isn't any more likely to end after high school than are digital natives likely to ditch their Facebook accounts once they turn eighteen. Whether you're a digital native or a "digital immigrant," who you are and how you express yourself online is now, and has since its inception been, entirely up to you—and that principle applies in the real world, too.

HEY BABY, WANNA SEE MY TIMELINE?

"GET IN! GET INTO THE *{BLEEPING}* BUS RIGHT *NOW!*"

I've been told that the Burning Man adventure starts at the moment you've decided to go, so perhaps it's unsurprising that I once found myself hitchhiking through a desolate stretch of Nevada desert with only a converted school bus driven by a very insistent stranger around to give me a lift. A friend and I had begun our journey in Denver a few days earlier, securing a rideshare in what turned out to be a fur-covered RV filled with an older group of so-called "Burners" before finding ourselves stranded in the desert when the RV got its second flat in as many days and we were suddenly stuck without transportation. After offloading all of our gear and fellow passengers into the cars of other Burners on their way to the week-long desert festival that prides itself on community, radical self-reliance and radical self-expression, we finally caught a ride for ourselves in the very surreal school bus with the very adamant driver ("Sorry," he said as we loaded up, "I just didn't want to be stopped in the middle of the road for long"). As soon as we pulled into Gerlach, the last town on the way to Black Rock City, the mid-desert home to Burning Man that exists for only one week out of every year, our overwhelmingly macho bus driver pulled over to the side of the road and broke out a bottle of brighter-than-bright red nail polish (and I do mean *bright*).

"Paint my nails, would you?" our handlebar-mustached, truck-driving, beer-bellied, alpha-male of a driver then asked as he popped open a beer and settled down to wait for the festival gates to open. "This is the only place I can wear nail polish without feeling like a *{bleep}*."

SEXY AND WE KNOW IT

While the maelstrom of radical, judgment-free self-expression that is Burning Man may encourage some of the wilder iterations of identity play known to mankind, you don't have to rough it in the desert for a week to know that ours has become a culture that values individuality. We sing along to the consistently morphing Lady Gaga as she tells us she was "Born This Way," watch reality TV shows that give us "Extreme Makeover(s)" and tell us "What Not to Wear," create virtual "Museum(s) of Me" and read books on how to "Become a Better You." So how did we progress from being a culture of Mr. Shoemakers and Mrs. Weavers into one full of Snookis, Madonnas, Stings and Fleas?

In the beginning, there were your parents. Who they were,

where they lived and what they did for a living were decided long before you were born and so, for that matter, was your own fate (as mentioned in chapter 1.2). You did what they did, you lived where they lived, and when you got old enough to marry and produce little yous, it was taken for granted that they too would do what you did and live where you lived. And so it went for generations, with identity being something decided by birthright, not desire. As society progressed and we went from villages to towns and cities, a bit of leeway started to appear, but it wasn't until the Industrial Revolution rolled around with its gales of mass employment and production that the historical tides began to shift permanently. The ability to experiment aesthetically, both in decorating yourself and decorating your home, was now able to reach into the newly formed middle class, no longer reserved for those born into wealthy households. An abundance of jobs and a flood of mass-produced goods now allowed millions of people to buy the same thing, giving birth to the prototypical Mr. and Mrs. Jones. More than just wanting to keep up with the Joneses, we wanted to *be* the Joneses—to show that we too could afford that toaster, that TV, that telephone.[99] Mass production had created a single, uniform concept of "normal" to which we could all aspire—for a little while, anyhow. Soon enough, one type of toaster gave way to ten, then to a hundred, and then to a thousand, and suddenly Mr. and Mrs. Jones were nowhere to be found in a marketplace flooded by choice after choice after choice after choice. The desire to be *normal* gave way to the desire to be *special*.

These days, mass customization is everywhere you look. There are more designers out there than ever before and design schools are overflowing with students looking to push that number up further still. While previous generations of designers sought to create one perfect version of an object, these days design is about helping each person find the object that's perfect for *them*.[100] And with so many endless iterations of each and every object and outfit now available online and at all price levels, it's getting harder and harder to settle for "just good enough" when we know that if we dig a bit further, we're bound to find "absolutely perfect."

The widespread cultural popularity of TV shows and books based on self-improvement and personal transformation reflects an understanding of the changing nature of modern identity, conscious or otherwise. Deep down, we've begun to feel the burden of creating our own identities for ourselves. We know that we can become a better version of ourselves if we put our minds to it; what we're not so quick to admit to is that who we are *is* who we've chosen to be, or at the very least who we've become by not choosing to be somebody else. We watch the televised transformations of others and imagine what it would be like to go through those same transformations ourselves. But rather than diving into big, difficult, life-changing personal revolutions—losing 50 pounds or quitting smoking or going from frumpy housewife to all-star diva—we focus on the part of our identity that's far easier to control: our outward appearance.

I KNOW YOU ARE
BUT WHAT AM I?

"No form of aesthetics matters more to us than personal appearance, the most inescapable sign of identity."

—*Virginia Postrel, political and cultural writer*[101]

So here we find ourselves, with a cultural emphasis on personal transformation; with both the freedom and the burden of creating our identities resting squarely on our own shoulders; with more options available across all spheres of life and at a cost affordable to just about anybody with a decent job; with a whole new online world in which we can express ourselves freely and connect with like-minded individuals doing the same; and with no historical examples as to how this is all supposed to play itself out. Here we now are, in the age of the individual and with the ability to choose for ourselves exactly who we want to be, yet with fingers ready to point at anybody who dares take the bait. Now what?

One of the key difficulties in creating your own identity lies in the fact that who you are now may not be anything like who you were ten years ago, or who you'll be in ten years from now. It's always been culturally acceptable to experiment with your identity while in school, but what happens when you become an adult and that experimentation continues? We are past the days when most adults worked for the same company for two or more decades; according to the Bureau of Labor Statistics, today's adults change jobs about every 4 years.[102] Nor are we likely to stay in the same home for too long; the US Census Bureau reports that the average American will move 12 times in a lifetime.[103] Add in all those diets, kids, makeovers and do-overs and it's clear that our adult identities have become more fluid than those of previous generations, causing us to continue some form of identity experimentation at a later point in life than was previously considered socially acceptable. What's more is that those past iterations of your identity are now preserved on social networks for all to see. Thankfully, I went through my dour-faced, XXL-t-shirt-wearing phase some years before Facebook and MySpace were invented, but today's kids won't be so lucky. And with Facebook actively promoting its new Timeline feature as a way to provide an online record of your life from birth, your emo phase could haunt you long after you trash your last Smiths album and burn the last of your oh-so-troubled high school poetry.

For the same reason that a macho bus driver I once met in a Nevada desert was unwilling to wear bright red nail polish anywhere but at a festival of self-expression, many of us are afraid to take our identity experimentation too far outside the boundaries of what we consider normal. But what *is* normal these days? When you've got thousands of possibilities for each your shirt, your pants, your shoes, your socks, your hair, your sunglasses, your jewelry, and every other part of what you might consider your typical outfit—not to mention your skin itself—who's to say that this outfit is normal, that outfit is passé, and those outfits are altogether outrageous? Who is the arbiter of style at a time when we're exposed to dozens, if not hundreds, of its iterations each and every day? And why the hell are we so offended by trends like skinny jeans anyways?

As society continues its relentless march towards rampant individuality, we're only likely to run into more modes of self-expression with every year that passes. The underlying reason why that guy you saw yesterday could feel comfortable wearing cut-off overalls with a bowtie and sock suspenders is the same reason that allows you to change jobs when the one you're at isn't cutting it anymore. In today's society, you can regularly adjust who you are based on who you really *want* to be—as can that guy with the sock suspenders. And the better you understand yourself, the better you're bound to understand others.[104] Rather than pointing the finger at those who take things "too far" (again, says who?), we ought to be pointing the finger at ourselves and asking, how far do I want to journey on the path to figuring out who I really want to be?

Each of us now has the freedom to be *exactly* who we choose to be. We are not forced into our identities, nor are we are forced to keep a single version of identity throughout our entire lives. We are free to choose—and so is everybody else. Likewise, we are free to judge others—and so is everybody else. Perhaps it's time we remember the golden rule rather than imposing our own belief system on others in a world where thousands of belief systems now have the freedom to peacefully coexist, and where we no longer possess a single overarching concept of "normal."

So what happens as these shifts in personal identity start following us into the workplace?

4 . . . THE LINE BETWEEN
LIFE AND WORK
IS CHANGING

TEXTS ON THE BEACH

It was a simple mix-up, really. He thought the meeting was on Thursday. The meeting was on Wednesday. So when Aleksej opened the fur-covered front door of his surreal office/apartment located in the heart of Berlin's Prenzlauer Berg, he did so half-naked, barefoot and wearing only a fuzzy blue robe that didn't leave much to the imagination. On the other side of the door stood the clients, two executives dressed in suits and sporting arched eyebrows and quizzical looks. Quickly realizing his mistake, Aleksej led the clients into the open kitchen area that also served as a conference room and asked them to take a seat at the table while he went and changed into something presentable.

Aleksej, a good friend of mine and the founder of an innovative event production company originally born from his penchant for projecting video at squat parties, then ducked into the bedroom located behind the main office while his clients waited in the kitchen/conference room and took in their wholly bizarre surroundings. The offices of Circus of Now have more in common with a museum than with a modern workplace, having been decorated and converted over the years by an equally distinctive Aleksej, 6'3", broad-shouldered and with intricate patterns shaved into his head and beard. More surprising than Aleksej, who they'd already met, or the office, which they'd already seen, was the object the clients now found lying in the middle of the kitchen table: a semi-automatic Walther PP pistol that happened to be resting on top of a Russian newspaper.

Having mixed up the date of the meeting, Aleksej saw no problem in having some friends over that Tuesday night. Among his guests was a close friend and coworker who also happened to collect decorative guns. He'd arrived the evening before to show off his new purchases, leaving the Walther PP behind after a thorough cleaning left it oily and unwieldy. So as not to stain the table, he'd left it on the closest newspaper he could find—a Russian one that Aleksej had just finished reading. It was there that the gun stayed until the next morning, when a now-dressed Aleksej reemerged into the kitchen to greet his now-mortified clients. So what does one do when his clients are seated for a conference with a freshly cleaned gun lying in the middle of the table?

"What else could I do?" recalls Aleksej. "I folded the other half of the newspaper over the gun and started the meeting." Not only did he still land the project—creating the event design for an important annual meeting and party—he would continue working with the client for another three years and through several more events. During that time, word of the gun incident would make its way around the client's office and Aleksej would become a local legend. Far from detracting from his reputation, it actually added to it. His became known as the company that could work under pressure—even with a gun resting conspicuously on the conference room table.*

THE BLACKBERRY BLUES

You don't have to be a pattern-bearded Berliner who lives in the company office to realize that sometimes, your work life and your personal life are bound to intersect in uncomfortable ways. As social networks and mobile technologies continue their meteoric rise in popularity, the concept of being able to leave work at the office and personal issues at home is fading further and further into obscurity. Whether we're checking our email on the beach or friending our coworkers at home, the life-work dichotomy has lately become anything but.

---

* Full disclosure: I used to work with Circus of Now.

LIFE, MEET WORK.
WORK, MEET LIFE.

US WORKERS WHO CHECK EMAIL DURING NON-OFFICE HOURS a

US WORKERS WHO CHECK EMAIL DURING HOLIDAYS b

DO SO MULTIPLE TIMES A DAY c

72%

68%

27%

82%

US EMPLOYEES WHO ADMIT TO USING PERSONAL SOCIAL NETWORKS IN THE OFFICE d

82% of Generation Y (aged 18-29 as of 2012) Facebook users have **at least 1 work friend**. **53% have more than 5** and **40% have more than 10**. Digital natives, whose views of social networks are more relaxed than those of previous generations, have yet to hit the workplace en masse. e

9 OUT OF 10 US HIRING MANAGERS USE SOCIAL NETWORKING TO SCREEN POTENTIAL CANDIDATES f

7 OUT OF 10 HAVE REJECTED CANDIDATES BECAUSE OF INFORMATION THEY FOUND ONLINE g

With social media having overtaken pornography as the #1 activity on the internet[105] and over half of all adults now toting internet-enabled smartphones,[106] there's no denying that we're increasingly connected to the internet and to each other, whether at home, at work or on the go. And when the same devices are being used for both work and play, it's getting harder and harder to separate one from the other—and increasingly, we don't.

> "Always On, Always Connected®"
> —*slogan for Research in Motion (RIM),*
> *makers of the BlackBerry*

In the pre-internet era, the different versions of your identity were easily compartmentalized. Beyond the annual company party or unexpectedly bumping into Ted from Marketing while at the grocery store, your work self and your personal self were very much separated. That separation was fueled by a very physical reality—being at work meant physically being at the office, with only the occasional personal phone call serving as an interruption. Likewise, once you physically left the office, the only reminders of your job came in the form of, "You won't believe what happened at work today, honey," or else the mental mulling over of tomorrow's big presentation.

The first fissures in the wall between life and work didn't appear until the mid-1990s, when the use of email in the workplace became widespread[107] and internet-connected computers began making their way into our homes. It took until 2001 for those computers to find their way into half of all American households, and with the increased reliance on email as a key form of work-related communication, companies began allowing employees to dial in remotely and check their email from home. Then came the email-enabled BlackBerry mobile, hitting 1 million subscribers by 2003[108] and forever changing the phrase "leave your work at the office." Consumer-level phones quickly hopped on the internet-enabled bandwagon and by the end of 2012, there are predicted to be more internet-enabled smartphones on the planet (10 billion) than there are human beings (7 billion).[109]

At the same time as smartphones were rising in popularity and our work email started following us beyond the office walls, at home we were experimenting with a more personal kind of technology—social networks. First there was Friendster in 2002, then there came MySpace in 2003, then Facebook in 2004, then Twitter in 2006, and within just a decade of the first true social network having hit the market, two-thirds of online adults were already using them.[110] Now let's step back from the technology for a moment and consider what this means. Within a matter of only ten years, the majority of our society has adopted a new set of tools largely based around sharing personal information, yet with a fundamental lack of understanding of the implications of doing so. Despite the fact that 90% of us admit to being concerned about online privacy,[111] we're obviously not concerned enough to log off altogether. And with social networking technology having been adopted in our personal lives prior to our work lives, unlike most technologies that preceded it, those privacy concerns carry very tangible real-world consequences. With the erosion of the line between life and work comes the erosion of the privacy boundaries that once separated the different parts of our lives. When you can check your work email during Thanksgiving dinner and post a picture of the turkey to Facebook where it can immediately be viewed and commented on by your best friend from college, your Auntie Mabel from Nantucket and Ted from Marketing, the different parts of your identity become harder and harder to differentiate. So what's an internet-connected, work-and-home-life-blurring girl to do?

ME (OR) ME (OR) ME

Back in 2009, I spent about five months living in Portugal. Though at the time my Facebook account was deactivated, I still got my social networking kick through my newly created (and entirely absurd) Twitter account. Rather than using it to post photos of my trip or interact with loved ones, I decided to use my first Twitter account to house what can be a very risqué sense of humor. For example:

Sophy Bot @sophybot   29 Sep 09
Dear mom: Today I learned how to say 'mother****er' in Portuguese. It was a good day. Love, Sophy

It took me about two months after that tweet to realize that my mom was, in fact, reading my Twitter account (despite not having an account of her own). Thankfully, she knows her daughter's sense of humor and was not offended, but it does beg a certain question: do we honestly know where the boundaries lie between the parts of our lives that are personal and the parts of our lives that are exposed to our family members and business colleagues? And better yet: do those boundaries even exist anymore?

Though the more lurid side of my internet presence may be offensive to some, others find it amusing, and ultimately it is a part of who I am and I don't want to hide the truth about myself any more than I want to invent a false identity. Now that the boundaries separating the different parts of our identities have come down and it's just as easy to find my raucously humored Twitter account as it is to find the straight-laced one I use to support this book project, the internet has exposed an interesting fact of our humanity: it turns out we are complex, multi-faceted individuals with wide arrays of interests and multiple ways of expressing ourselves in different contexts. And therein lies the problem with the disappearing boundaries: context.

When I wrote the above tweet, I did so within a given context—in this case, a set of followers familiar with my risqué humor and looking for jokes, not practical updates. Similarly, when I update my book-related Twitter handle, I do so with information related to this project. To tweet a dirty joke to my book followers would be to take it out of context, rendering it not only irrelevant, but probably inappropriate. But on Facebook, where our posts are tied to our real names and where we maintain a single identity whether connecting with current colleagues or old college buddies, the concept of context becomes more difficult to discern. And with friends having the ability to tag you in their photos or to post those photos somewhere else altogether, you're not the only one in control of your identity. Though you may be ok with a certain silly photo appearing in a casual social context, there's no guarantee it will stay there.

TALKIN' 'BOUT MY REPUTATION

In a highly publicized 2006 lawsuit involving social networking privacy issues,[112] then 25-year-old high school teacher Stacy Snyder suffered the repercussions of posting a photo to her MySpace profile that seemed to her, at the time, to be fairly innocuous. Sporting a pirate hat and drinking from a plastic cup, she'd labeled the photo "Drunken Pirate." While her friends had a laugh, the supervisor at her school proved unamused. Snyder was fired and lost her court appeal, despite her claim that the party had taken place off-campus and after-hours. What was an acceptable social indiscretion for a 25-year-old in one context became an unforgivable breach of policy in another, and Snyder's reputation as a teacher was ruined.

There may be privacy settings out there to keep your photos away from public eyes, but as the technology continues to develop at a breakneck pace and sites like Pinterest can gain 10 million new users within just 9 months,[113] the technology is developing faster than the etiquette. Nor are the sites particularly encouraging you to read through their lengthy, jargon-filled privacy policies. Signing up for a Facebook account requires you to read only 63 words before clicking the "Sign Up" button. Among those 63 words, you're told that clicking that button stipulates your agreement to their terms and data policy—a suite of separate web pages that adds up to over 11,000 words (a third of the length of this book). In the interest of convenience, we sign up anyways and trade away our privacy, forgetting about the potential issues until the moment when a problem arises. We want free email from Google, so we allow our messages to be scanned so it can target appropriate ads at us. We want our iPhones to help us find the nearest Starbucks, so we let Apple keep track of everywhere we go. We want to find our friends on Facebook, so we upload our address books to be scanned and filed. This wonderfully convenient modern life of ours comes at the cost of personal information that has been private for the whole of human history. So what do we do about it?

When 7 out of 10 hiring managers admit to rejecting job candidates because of information found online, our web-based reputations are obviously important. Every week, new articles hit the web about separating your work life from your private life online, and "best practices" disseminated by colleges and institutions encourage you to minimize or delete your social media presence altogether.[114] But what happens if your kids post about how "mom got fired" or "OMG dad fell asleep drunk on the sofa ROFL!"? And what happens when we acknowledge the fact that online data traces often have the permanence of tattoos, meaning I can still find the results of an online Simpsons quiz I filled out when I was 15 or a starry-eyed U2 concert review I posted at 17? Can we continue to deny the reality of our multi-faceted humanity, able to party with your decorative-gun-toting friends one night and win over the client's approval the next morning?

As the line between public figure and private citizen gets as blurry as the line between your work identity and your social identity, it's no wonder entrepreneurs love touting the concept of a meritocracy. Nobody wants to be told who they should be or how they should act, or to completely curtail one of the most exciting parts of modern life in fear of being judged out of context. Denying the complexity of our humanity will only work for so much longer. Soon enough, we'll have to admit that sometimes, even the guy with the gun on the conference table can still be good at his job. And soon enough, employers will have to admit it too.

THE PARADOX OF THE PRODUCTIVE PUNK

IT TOOK AN ENTIRE DECADE of struggling with the structure of an enzyme produced by an AIDS-like virus before scientists decided to throw the problem to an unlikely set of collaborators—online gamers. It took the gamers only three weeks to solve it.

Produced by the University of Washington in 2008, Foldit is an online puzzle game where players compete to unfold chains of amino acids. When the enzyme from the Mason-Pfizer monkey virus was added to the game, players were quickly able to produce a valid protein shape that researchers then verified as correct. The results were published in the Nature Structural & Molecular Biology journal in late 2011,[115] marking the first time that gamers and scientific researchers were simultaneously acknowledged as co-authors.

Of the 240,000 players registered on Foldit,[116] few have any background in the field of biochemistry on which the game is based. So how were they able to rapidly solve a problem in a field they knew nothing about? The answer lies in the mechanics of game design and the chemistry of the human brain. By converting a scientific problem into a puzzle with easy-to-understand rules and pitting players against one another on a point-based leaderboard, games like Foldit take real-world problems out of the realm of *work* and put them firmly into the realm of *fun*. The pressure to solve the puzzle doesn't come from a boss or authority figure, but instead from the player himself. For the same reason kids are late to dinner because "c'mon mom, I just have to beat one more bad guy to get to the next level," players don't want to stop until they solve the next problem.

The chemical reason why we keep going is directly tied to the neurotransmitter dopamine, which—to grossly oversimplify—is a brain chemical that makes you feel good. Dopamine is the stuff that's released when you're listening to a good song, eating a good meal or having good sex. It's also the stuff that's released when you're gambling or playing a video game. Studies have shown that the near-miss—almost winning, but not quite—triggers a higher level of dopamine than does constant winning.[117] The result? "Just one more try mom, *please.*" By harnessing the power of games to tap into our brain's hardwired reward centers, Foldit's creators discovered a way to make real-world problems fun to solve. And they're far from the only ones who've done so.

TIME TO PLAY
YOUR HOMEWORK, DEAR

The word may not have hit the Oxford Dictionary yet, but that hasn't stopped venture capitalists from investing $25 million in the newly invented field of gamification, "the use of game design techniques and mechanics to solve problems and engage audiences."[118] The US Navy is using it to fight real-world Somali pirates,[119] Marriott[120] and PepsiCo[121] are using it to find and hire new employees, and even Nobel Laureate Al Gore, citing that "games are the new normal," is challenging design firms to create a gamified way of spreading the word about climate change.[122] At the heart of these developments is a simple question: why can't work be fun? Challenging the traditional notion of work and school as boring-yet-necessary lifetime ordeals, the burgeoning gamification industry—expected to grow to $2.8 billion by 2015[123]—is hoping to revolutionize the way we learn and the way we do our jobs.

> "I have never let my schooling interfere with my education."
> —*Mark Twain*

A 2007 survey of 81,000 high school students across 26 states found that a whopping 2 out of 3 of them felt bored in class every single day.[124] Whether they blamed it on the school, on the teachers or on the curriculum, a big part of the problem lies in the fact that the one-size-fits-all, one-way lecture model of education is out of step with the world outside of the classroom. In his 2008 book *Grown Up Digital*,

Don Tapscott noted that, "the model of education that still prevails today was designed for the Industrial Age... The student, working alone, is expected to absorb the content delivered by the teacher."[125] Those same students then go home and plug into the interactive, many-to-many content and communication models that drive the internet. They produce, create and interact with new content on a daily basis and, given the level playing field that is the internet, ambitious kids can now release apps, create sites, blog, and find other ways to start their first company long before they take their first college class. When school can earn good grades but the internet can earn cold, hard cash, gaining the teacher's respect just doesn't feel as important. Whether in school or at the office, the traditional hierarchies of past generations are beginning to come apart at the seams.

HIERARCHY SCHMIERARCHY

When I first graduated college and hit the workforce, I was one of those bright-eyed, bushy-tailed recent grads ready to go out and change the world for the better. My first full-time office job started out simply enough, with me doing as I was told and staying mum even when a task struck me as illogical. Overachiever that I am, that didn't last for long. Soon enough I started approaching my managers with proposed solutions to what I recognized as actionable problems, and it was then that I realized my managers fell into two distinct categories: the one that heard me out and took my considerations seriously, and the one that was bound to respond, "but we've always done it this way." I inadvertently ignited a schism through my constant questions and suggestions, rallying the one category of managers who happily let me solve problems when I proved capable of doing so, and frustrating the other who openly objected to allowing a newcomer like me to institute company-wide changes. In the end, I quit both the job and the full-time office world, unwilling to cope with the second category of managers for the same reason that others in my generation take for granted the coming collapse of longevity-based hierarchies: I wanted to work based on my ability, not on my age or the length of my tenure.

Those of us in Generation Y and younger grew up in a world that rewarded successful youth. We watched the dot-com boom turn our peers into millionaires. We heard story after story of young company founders striking internet gold. We saw Marc Zuckerberg become one of the wealthiest men in the world. The success stories we observed were based on hard work and good ideas, implanting in each of us the realization that, given an idea of our own backed by the necessary effort, there was nothing preventing us from joining their ranks. With decreased startup costs for internet-based companies and increased amounts of venture capitalists ready to fund the hell out of them, we saw opportunity in the world around us, and willingly sidestepped any obstacle that stood in our way. To us, job loyalty means giving our company the best we've got, and has little to do with how long we actually work there.

"We live in a free and open society, but many of our workplace organizations use the command-and-control style."
—*Asher Adelmen, President, Workplace Democracy Association*[126]

With the majority of us now participating in leadership-decentralized social networks that operate as a circle of equals, it's little wonder that the younger among us have difficulty adjusting to the entrenched hierarchies that we encounter in the business world—ones that bear a closer resemblance to pyramids than to circles. To get things done in a circle of experts, you find the person with the appropriate area of expertise and assign them the appropriate task. Getting things done in a pyramidal structure isn't as cut-and-dry. Do you assign the task to the manager, who will then assign it to the subordinate, possibly losing valuable information in the process of translation? Or do you go directly to the subordinate, possibly creating waves by bypassing the manager? The difficulty here is that the circular structure is the one we're accustomed to dealing with in our personal lives; its rules make sense to us and we know how it operates. The pyramidal structure, on the other hand—not so much.

The ability to create and distribute content in our personal lives has imbued today's youth with a certain managerial mind-set. We know how to solve certain problems and get certain things done. But when we hit the workplace and find that it follows a wholly different set of rules that doesn't fit with the system we're familiar with, we run into trouble. Nor do we rebel because we're trying to be difficult. With the constant arrival of new technologies that has become the hallmark of modern life, we've developed a certain systems-analysis mindset when it comes to deciphering how to use them. We bring that same mindset to school and to work, looking for the best way to solve a problem with little regard as to how others solved it in the past. We're obstinate not because of rebellion, but because we've grown accustomed to solving problems for ourselves in whichever way seems the most logical. And at a time when the internet has allowed us to question the official story about anything, we're no longer willing to blindly accept "because I said so" as an answer.

The iron-clad rules of many traditional hierarchies strike the internet generation as unnecessary and undesirable. We are used to multitasking and prioritizing at school and in our homes, and we want to be able to do the same at our jobs. At the opposite end of our expectations lies one of my own relatives—a senior employee with over 25 years of experience and over a decade spent with his current company—who still has to ask his boss if he needs to leave work 15 minutes early to go to a doctor's appointment (despite the fact that he regularly comes in early, takes work home, doesn't miss deadlines and is one of the most highly respected people in his department). Post-Industrial Revolution hierarchical organizations thus had a tendency to treat their employees like children incapable of making their own decisions, and many companies still do so (a 2008 poll of nearly 2,500 employees found that 25% of working Americans view their workplace as a dictatorship).[127] When a highly respected, highly competent employee is unable to decide for himself when it is OK to leave the office a few minutes early, something is definitely out of whack.

A meta-analysis of 25 studies found that as power levels within an organization increase, evaluations of subordinates become increasingly negative.[128] At the same time, studies have shown that employees who identify with their organization do a better job.[129] For today's younger employees, and for the next generation of employees set to hit the workplace, job loyalty will not be based on hierarchical structures that encourage negativity, but on alignment with the company's objectives and the freedom to work towards them. That doesn't mean we won't have bosses. It means those bosses will have the same goals as we do and will trust us to do our best in attaining them.

When crowdsourced knowledge database Wikipedia first came out, people were quick to assume that it wouldn't work. After all, why would anybody want to contribute work anonymously and without a tangible reward? Some eleven years later, our fears proved unfounded. Despite the occasional prankster, Wikipedia has shown a better side of our humanity—one that it is concerned with real knowledge and real facts, and one that is more interested in sharing the truth than in playing around with falsehoods. When hierarchical workplaces belittle us in the interest of controlling us, they deny this fact. Just ask any kid which parental admonishment hurts more: "You're punished" or "I'm disappointed." Perhaps, given the ability to do so, we'd rather work hard and be successful than fool around and do nothing. All we need to do now is agree on the parameters.

9ISH TO 5ISH

2:45 AM.

"GET UP!" MY ALARM CLOCK INSISTS. "Get up from your nap! The call's about to start!"

Reluctantly I do so, heading to the kitchen for a glass of water before returning to the floor-bound pillow in front of my "desk," a shin-high table slapped together from scrap wood left over when the previous tenants of my loft discovered an empty pop-up room above their apartment and built a set of stairs to access it. Completely lacking insulation and a laughably far cry from any sort of room that might some day pass a building inspection, this is the space I rent in Bushwick shortly after I quit my office job and leave my married yuppie lifestyle behind while I try to figure out what to do next.

2:50 AM.

Ten minutes ahead of my scheduled 3AM conference call, I plop down on the floor of my illegally built pop-up room in the far reaches of Bushwick, Brooklyn, don a headset, rev up

GoToMeeting, and wait silently for the other callers to join the session. Less than ten yards from where I sit, a group of nighttime revelers is hanging out on the building's rooftop, chatting and socializing as I hear a ping and thank the first caller for joining.

2:55 AM.

"So how's the weather in Beijing?" I ask into my headset, making idle chit-chat as I wait for the rest of the attendees to join the meeting.

As the clock strikes 3:00 and a final ping informs me that the last attendee has arrived, I open up the remote meeting application, share my screen, and proceed to lead an hour-long training session on business recovery and crisis management procedures with half a dozen managers located across three of my client's locations in China. Once the call is finished, I shut down GoToMeeting before crawling out of my window and onto the graffiti-covered rooftop, joining the nearby revelers for a little nightcap.

My new consulting job never ceases to amaze me.

WIN/WIN/WORK FROM HOME

Ah, freelance. When I first left my office job, I could never have envisioned the absurd scenarios my resulting telecommuting lifestyle would soon unleash. It was the newfound ability to work remotely that sent me traveling across the US and Western Europe, armed with a backpack full of portable technology and the flames of wanderlust licking at my feet. Unlike my office job, my new consulting gig allowed me to work based on my ability and to set my own rules for how to do so. As long as I produced good work, submitted my hours honestly and strictly adhered to any provided deadlines, my new company couldn't have cared less if I was right down the street or halfway across the world. While my office job had so often admonished me when I tried to push too far, my new job both encouraged and rewarded my input. Their trust made me proud, and I worked harder still. Though I was more often to be found working at 2AM than I was at 9, my new job didn't care. I had been rewarded with the freedom to work my own way, no matter how bizarre my working habits appeared, and in return I gave them the very best that I had. It was a win/win situation and I, like so many others who have left the 9-to-5 environment not out of laziness but out of a bullheaded unwillingness to work by rules we don't agree with, vowed never to take another job that was more interested in my outfit than my output.

While the jury's still out on just how many telecommuters there are out there, with numbers varying depending on the source, everybody does agree that telecommuting is definitely on the rise (one recent study predicts that 60% of UK workers could regularly be working from home within a decade).[130] And though many managers still worry that "how do I know they're working?," several studies now show that not only are they working, they're more productive and happier while doing it.

Researchers at Stanford University recently partnered with a Chinese travel agency interested in implementing a telecommuting program involving over 12,000 employees. After conducting a survey to determine willingness and suitability, 255 employees were chosen to begin the program. Within just a few weeks, the telecommuters were already shown to be out-performing their office-bound colleagues, taking more calls, working more hours and requiring fewer sick days.[131] A 2011 survey of 140 telecommuters conducted by Staples revealed that 86% of respondents reported being more productive when working from home. Respondents also pointed to a 25% drop in stress levels when compared to working at the office, and 80% reported an improvement in their work-life balance.[132] Another study published in the Journal of Applied Communication Research in 2010 also revealed telecommuting employees showing higher job satisfaction and an improvement in work-life balance over their on-site counterparts.[133]

The sum of these studies goes against the command-and-control managerial style of generations past, showing that many employees operate more effectively when left to manage themselves. And while not all jobs can be performed from home and not all employees want to do so in the first place, these studies do reveal that sometimes, for some employees, telecommuting is absolutely the right way to go. Heeding this revelation is not so much a matter of unleashing all employees to go upgrade their home offices, but rather pinpointing those who are most likely to create the win/win scenario of both higher productivity and higher job satisfaction. As for those left in the office, a whole other set of studies points to their version of the win/win working arrangement—and you might be surprised at the seemingly distracting situations that ultimately result in higher productivity.

BEST. STUDIES. EVER.

Have you ever tried convincing your boss to buy 500 multi-colored glow-in-the-dark bouncy balls?

Let me explain. I once helped organize a big event whose theme was "The Ball," not in reference to a gala but to a 9-foot-diameter inflatable projection surface that was to be suspended in the middle of the room, and it was then that I found myself in front of my boss with one of those Oriental Trading catalogs in my hand and an ear-to-ear grin on my face. For less than a hundred bucks, I told him, we could pop a couple of glow-in-the-dark bouncy balls into each of the gift bags that would be distributed to the attendees. They matched the theme, I said, would put a smile on people's faces, and the cost was pretty much negligible in terms of the event overall. And wouldn't you know it, he actually agreed.

The bulk pricing had left us with a bunch of extras, most of which quickly disappeared onto our desks and into our pockets. While the event itself was a success, what happened afterwards was an unexpected bonus. The bouncy balls first made an appearance at the after-party, pulled out of our pockets and bounced through the crowds among us coworkers. They were there in the office the next day, bouncing from desk to desk and being used as stress balls during lengthy calls. They followed us even when we left the office, pulled out as a joke before and after meetings, lightening our moods and reminding us of the heavy teamwork it took to pull off events like the one we'd just finished. Though I'd never expected my boss to agree to the purchase in the first place, even more surprising was the lasting effect it had on our office. For months to come, the glow-in-the-dark bouncy balls were pretty much guaranteed to make us smile whenever they happened to emerge. They reminded us that we were a team, and that together we could get big things done.

Studies have long since proven the harmful effects of negative emotions when it comes to our mental performance. More recently, research has shown the opposite to be true—positive emotions lead to improved performance. Whether we're being funny, friendly or nice, these positive emotions have been shown to provide not only tangible cognitive benefits, but an actual increase in productivity. And now, some science:

(1) Researchers at Northwestern University tested the ability of participants to solve word puzzles after watching a short comedy routine. They found participants were more likely to solve a puzzle when attempting it right after watching the routine. Mark Beeman, a neuroscientist involved in the study, reflected that, "what we think is happening is that the humor, this positive mood, is lowering the brain's threshold for detecting weaker or more remote connections." The more

connections we see, the better we get at solving puzzles.[134]

(2) At the University of Copenhagen, participants were asked to perform a simple task—watching videos of people passing balls and counting the passes—after first being presented with a distraction. Some participants were shown a comedy video while the rest were shown a button that would display a comedy video if clicked, but told to refrain from doing so. Ten minutes then elapsed while some of the participants were heard laughing at the video and the rest sat and waited. When it was time to perform the task itself, those who had watched the funny video were found to be more efficient, making significantly fewer mistakes than those who hadn't.[135]

(3) A study out of the Warwick Business School presented similar findings in the "watch funny video --> perform cognitive task" category of research. Their study had some participants watch a 10-minute video of a famous British comedian while others watched a "placebo" video featuring colored patterns. After being asked to rate their happiness levels, participants were told to perform a series of simple math exercises. The workers who rated themselves as happier were found to be 12% more productive, while the unhappier workers were 10% *less* productive.[136]

(4) An unrelated study out of the University of Michigan tested the ability of participants to play brain games (such as word puzzles) following various types of social interactions. Their findings demonstrated that those who'd had a brief friendly conversation with another person subsequently performed better on an array of cognitive tasks, while those

who'd had a competitive-spirited conversation showed no such improvement. The conversations, incidentally, had nothing to do with the task at hand.[137]

(5) A 2000 study by Yale University and the Center for Socialization and Development – Berlin similarly reported the benefits associated with positive emotions, this time when tied to leadership. The study concluded that the most successful leaders among its participants, whether CEOs or PTA leaders, were those who treated subordinates with respect and made a genuine effort to be liked.[138]

> "People rarely succeed unless they have fun in what they are doing."
> —*Dale Carnegie, management guru*

Ok, so we're better at our jobs when we're feeling good or when we've just been amused by something funny. But what about all that idle internet-surfing? An Australian study by the University of Melbourne found that 70% of the 300 workers involved engaged in leisure internet-browsing while at work. It also found that those employees were 9% *more* productive than those who abstained.[139] Finally, a study by the National University of Singapore assigned participants a series of tasks punctuated by a 10-minute break. One group spent the break on a filler task, a second was free to do anything but surf the internet, and the third was allowed to surf a pre-selected group of internet sites featuring news, social networking, gaming and entertainment. Following another set of tasks, the internet-surfing group was found to be 16% more productive than the rest-break group and 39% more productive than the control group.[140] In the words of the LA Times: "best study ever."[141]

At the heart of all these studies is an exciting revelation. Researchers are repeatedly demonstrating that, despite conventional management techniques that say otherwise, we're better at our jobs, more productive, and happier to boot when we're allowed to act like the multi-faceted human beings we are and not the task-oriented drones our jobs often want us to be. Yes, say the studies, you really do work better when you're in a good mood. Yes, they say, you'll do better if you're allowed to take YouTube or Facebook breaks. No, they say, working from home doesn't make you less efficient, but more so. Yes, they say, being nice and having occasional friendly conversations really can lead to higher success rates.

Now obviously this is just a handful of studies, but the growing body of evidence is hard to ignore—we perform better in a kinder, more flexible work environment. Two out of three digital natives think that "working and having fun can and should be the same thing."[142] That doesn't mean they're looking for a free ride or an easy way out, but that they honestly believe that the work itself can be enjoyable. Whether it's gamification, telecommuting, looser restrictions on what is and isn't allowed in the workplace, or just plain old being allowed to be yourself and have fun while getting things done, the future of work is beginning to shift. And I, for one, welcome our new fun-loving overlords.

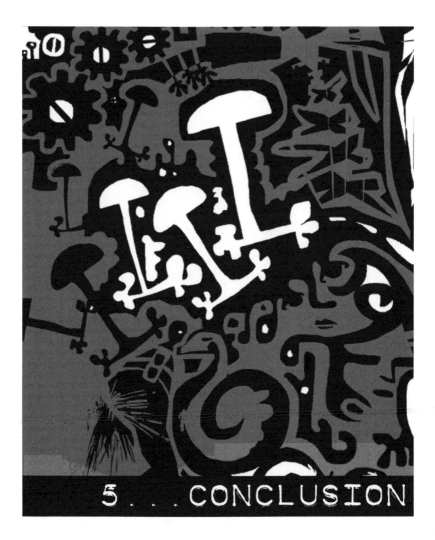

5...CONCLUSION

HIPSTER? I HARDLY KNOW HER!

ABOUT A YEAR INTO THIS PROJECT, I sat in the most hipster of all possible hipster places—a bar on Bedford Avenue in Williamsburg, Brooklyn—and told a friend that I thought the word "hipster" had become a misnomer and I was working on a book to try and prove as much. *"Shhh...."* he whispered, immediately cutting me off and nervously looking around to see if anybody had heard me. *"You shouldn't use that word in here."*

As elusive as a unicorn yet as common as an ant, the hipster seems to be everywhere and nowhere at once. Those of us who have been called hipsters hate that somebody associated us with *those types*, yet most of us are guilty of having used the word on others. Calling somebody a hipster is tantamount to saying, "you're annoying, you try way too hard, your attitude sucks, and you're completely superficial," yet anybody wearing a thick-rimmed set of glasses is assumed to be one. We've come to associate this extremely negative set of personality traits with an extremely common set of fashion trends, but how often do those traits and trends actually exist in tandem?

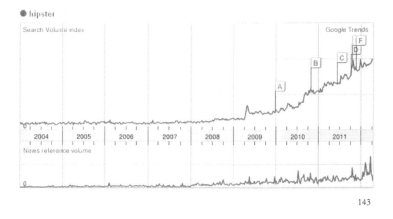

143

Although some articles declared them dead as early as 2003, this chart showing the amount of people searching Google for the word "hipster" tells a very different story. It tells the story of the popularization of a word; of its increased usage; of the fact that more and more people out there are being associated with all the negative traits carried by that word. It tells the story of a growing stereotype, one based not on gender or on race, but on how a person outwardly chooses to express their personality. An overwhelming minority of people out there use the word positively—for the most part, we all agree that we hate them. So if we despise and vilify hipsters so much, why are they *increasing* in popularity? If nobody wants to be called a hipster and we all hate who they are and what they represent, why on earth would *more* people willingly turn into them? The answer is pretty simple, if you think about it: it's not that there are more of these annoyingly superficial hipsters out there than there used to be. We're just using the *word* more. And that means we're insulting more and more people who are doing nothing more than expressing themselves in a way that our society has otherwise come to accept.

Now that we're past the days when your identity was defined by where you were born and who your parents were, it's up to each of us to create an identity of our own. We do so with the things that we wear, the people we associate with, the places we go and the things that we like. The problem we've run into is one of interpretation—I think this outfit means one thing, but you think it means something else entirely. Back in the day, people knew exactly what it meant to wear a pair of Vans sneakers—it meant you were a skater. But once Vans increased in popularity and became available in every mall across America, wearing them could make you a skater to one person, a poser to the next, a punk rocker to the third, an emo to the fourth, and so on. We no longer share a universal set of meanings about the items we choose to wear and without that shared meaning, interpreting what that kid over there is trying to say with his washed-out Slayer shirt is anyone's guess.

When you can find 3,600 types of something as simple as a toothbrush on Amazon (and 3,800 types of toothpaste), people start to wonder why you chose *that* particular toothbrush and *that* particular toothpaste. A rechargeable Philips Sonicare and a tube of Tom's of Maine's Fluoride-Free Peppermint? What, you're too good for a simple bristle job and a bottle of Colgate? The more intimate the items are to our sense of self, the more harshly we tend to judge them. *Look at that loser in the fedora over there. He's such a f******* hipster.*

Meanwhile, maybe that guy is wearing that fedora because his grandfather just passed away and left it to him since he'd always tried it on as a kid. Or maybe his girlfriend gave it to him and he trusted her when she said he looked good in it. Or maybe—just maybe—he simply felt like wearing a fedora today. Maybe he wasn't trying to send any signals. Maybe he just woke up and decided it was a fedora kinda day. The point is that we no longer know. The time in our society when we all shared one single meaning for something like a fedora hat is long since gone. Placing your judgment on somebody else based on your interpretation is just that— you are placing your judgment on somebody else. So when you assume that the kid over there is wearing his Slayer shirt ironically without knowing that he's actually going through a metalhead phase and that happens to be his favorite band at the moment, you'd be totally off-base in calling him a hipster. You would, in fact, be stereotyping him.

"But what about the whole 'I liked them before they were cool' thing that hipsters say?" you may ask. "Doesn't that prove they're judgmental jerks?"

First off, I have to say that I've honestly never heard anybody using that particular statement, and I doubt many people have actually heard it first-hand. The more likely statement is something akin to, "I liked their first album better," which we then assume to mean that this person is declaring that they liked that band (or movie or object or trend) before it was well known, hence being cool enough to know about it before *you*.

I have a confession to make: I did actually like LCD Soundsystem's first album better. Now before you go break out the torches and pitchforks, let me explain. You see, when I first heard LCD Soundsystem, their sound was novel to me. I enjoyed its novelty and ended up listening to its songs countless times over the course of the next year. By the time their second album came out, I had built up a certain set of expectations for what I wanted to hear from this band I'd come to love. And the truth is, the album just didn't meet the high expectations I'd set, nor was it different enough to bring back the novelty factor that had attracted me to them in the first place. Anyways, in the time since their first album had come out, I'd been exposed to dozens of other bands in my day-to-day internet travels, many of which attracted me because of *their* novelty factor. Unfortunately, if I ever tell anybody my honest opinion about which LCD Soundsystem album I enjoyed the most, their resulting opinion about me will be simple: *hipster.*

THAT'S ALL, FOLKS

So here's the thing: by now, you've probably decided I'm a hipster. Bummer. But by no means am I trying to defend those jerks out there who think they are cooler than you; those trust-fund babies who spend their days talking about art projects they never get around to starting; those passionless jerks who only like things ironically and who think you're pathetic for liking them sincerely. What I'm trying to say here is that the people who actually fit all of those (genuinely) negative traits that we associate with the word "hipster" are by far and large in the minority. Most of the people we call hipster *aren't*. We tend to use the word on anybody who looks like they're trying harder to be cool than we are. But with so many endless options out there for expressing ourselves, who's to say why a person *really* dresses the way they do? Are they honestly trying so hard to be cool, or are they just wearing that crazy outfit because they *can*?

As kids, we play dress-up and nobody seems to mind. Sometimes we dress up as superheroes and princesses because that's who we'd really like to be, but sometimes we just put on anything we can find for no other reason than the aesthetic pleasure that it gives us. When we're younger, it's ok to experiment with our appearance. When we're older, suddenly that makes us hipsters, and since we consider all hipsters to be scumbags, experimenting with your appearance suddenly makes you a scumbag. Why? Why does it offend people so badly when somebody wants to wear something a bit outlandish? Why do we assume that must mean they're judging us for not doing the same, so we preemptively judge them as hipsters so we can automatically discount their own (most likely nonexistent) judgment? If Jimi Hendrix were to walk down Bedford Avenue right now, would he honestly be called anything but a hipster?

Ours has become the most open society to ever exist, period. We have more options available across all spheres of life than anybody in history could possibly have even dreamed of, and we have the freedom to explore them at will. We have access to all the different elements of our culture, and the freedom to choose exactly which ones we want to pursue. We are free to be ourselves, to do our own thing and, increasingly, even to work on our own terms. For the most part, we're just plain old free. Rather than judging one another while we curiously experiment with these freedoms, exploring facets and elements of our society that have long since lost their original meanings, we really ought to take a step back and appreciate all of this newfound freedom. The most beautiful part of our wide-open, post-internet, option-filled, filtered-for-your-browsing-pleasure society is that we are now free to choose *exactly* how we want to live and who we want to be—and so, it's worth remembering, is everybody else.

ACKNOWLEDGMENTS

For all its final brevity, this project was quite the doozy, spanning twenty months spent living across three states and with two solo cross-country drives nestled somewhere in between. At some point along the way I got a puppy, who I'd like to acknowledge first here, but seeing as he can't read anyways I think I'll just get him a big old beef knuckle to thank him for putting up with so many countless utterances of, "not now, sweetheart, mommy's busy."

And now, on to my human compatriots (in no particular order).

To my editor, Rick Raguso, much obliged. Despite my crazy timeline and a hefty dose of anxiousness, you stayed cool and helped me get it done. Thank ye kindly, good sir.

To Mr. Infographic himself, Thiago Demello Bueno: thanks for the awesome work you did on these, and beyond that, thanks for all the encouragement along the way. Yer a real pal, Thiago.

Hey João Raposo Portuguese Artiste! Thank you for the utterly amazing work you did on the cover and the section images. Shpektakular, my friend—really. Fixe.

To my mom and my stepdad, Tanya and Mike Gertsik, thank you for being so supportive throughout this whole project, even when that meant physically putting up with both me and my enormous puppy. Sorry about the scratched-up floors (and thanks again)!

A huge thank you goes to my over-the-fence friend Oz (James L. Osborn Jr. to be formal about it), though we never did figure out which one of us was supposed to be Wilson. Our innumerable conversations helped me tighten my arguments and stay inspired even when I was dying to take a break. Really, Oz—I cannot thank you enough for all your wise and kind words.

Yo, Teach! A big mountainous thank you to Mr. Frank Reetz and his 2010-2011 sixth grade class at West Jefferson Middle School in Conifer, CO. Thanks for believing in me Frank, and thanks for giving me the opportunity to talk with your wonderful students!

Vielen dank to my good friend Aleksej Schoen for helping me out with his gun-toting story, and more importantly for helping me start on this identity-defining journey back in my yuppie days when I had no idea that work could actually be fun and I could actually be myself while doing it. You opened my eyes to something that I hadn't even realized was possible. Spasibo, Aleksej.

Many thanks to the lovely crew of Lootok for letting me swoop in and nab billable hours every time the realization came that, "wait, it's taking longer to finish than I thought." A special thank you to

Iris Chung (Dearest Miss P'eye) for writing my bio, to Roberta Trentin for taking some great press photos, and to Mr. Sean Murphy himself for so sincerely believing in me. My humble thanks.

Dearest Andrew and Morgan Sispoidis, two of my biggest encouragers and fans, a very pointed tip o' the hat to yis. Throughout the myriad times when everybody else said I was crazy, you two were sure to exclaim, "ooh, that sounds really interesting!" For that, I truly thank you.

To Velibor Pedevski, for always pushing me to keep going, keep going, keep going, get it done. I finally did, v. Thanks for kicking my ass into gear whenever I needed it.

To my dad, Zinovy Shnaper, who I promised to acknowledge when he got me a desk on which to work on this project (HA told you I'd remember) and also, y'know, coz he's my dad.

To John Clay and Mitch Riesling for more recently housing me and the pup (despite already having SEVEN hounds in the house), and for dealing with my borderline shut-in status as I've worked on finishing this up and getting it out there. Much obliged, gents.

And finally, to all of the other lovely people out there who've encouraged me, helped me, and just generally put up with my endless ramblings as I slowly navigated my way through this unexpectedly intensive project—thank you! Without all of the encouragement along the way, I don't know if I would've been able to finish it. Mental hugs for everybody!

WORKS CITED

1.   Heffel, Lesley. "How Many Hipsters Does It Take to Secede from Brooklyn?" Web log post. *Brooklyn Skeptic.* 5 July 2007. Web. <http://brooklynskeptic.wordpress.com/2007/07/05/how-many-hipsters-does-it-take-to-secede-from-brooklyn/>.

2.   Haddow, Douglas. "Hipster: The Dead End of Western Civilization." *Adbusters* 29 July 2008. Web. <http://www.adbusters.org/magazine/79/hipster.html>.

3.   Borow, Zev. "Will The Last Hipster Please Turn Out The Lights?" *New York Guides.* New York Magazine, 21 May 2005. Web. <http://nymag.com/nymetro/urban/features/10488/>.

4.   Moss, J. Jennings. "Dude, "Hipster" Is So 2008." Web log post. *Portfolio.com.* American City Business Journals, 13 Jan. 2011. Web. <http://www.portfolio.com/views/blogs/entrepreneurship/2011/01/13/san-francisco-startup-names-itself-hipster/>.

5.   Da Silva, Kerry. "Why Hipsters Suck." *Hybrid Magazine.* Sept. 2002. Web. <http://www.hybridmagazine.com/culture/0902/dasilva.shtml>.

6.   See #5

7.   Idan. "Stalking the Wild Hipster." *Everything2.* Everything2 Media, LLC, 9 Nov. 2004. Web. <http://everything2.com/title/Stalking+the+Wild+Hipster>.

8.   "Hipster." *Cracked.com.* Demand Media, Inc. Web. <http://www.cracked.com/funny-4573-hipster/>.

9. Parasuco, Trey. "Hipster." *Urban Dictionary.* Urban Dictionary, 22 Nov. 2007. Web. <http://www.urbandictionary.com/define.php?term=hipster>.

10. Fletcher, Dan. "Hipsters." *Time Magazine* 29 July 2009. Web. <http://www.time.com/time/arts/article/0,8599,1913220,00.html>.

11. Anderson, Jon. "Prohibition Was Never This Funny." *Chicago Tribune* 23 Sept. 1985. Print.

12. Sagert, Kelly Boyer. *Flappers: A Guide to an American Subculture.* Santa Barbara, CA: Greenwood, 2010. Print.

13. See #12

14. Sann, Paul. *The Lawless Decade; a Pictorial History of a Great American Transition: From the World War I Armistice and Prohibition to Repeal and the New Deal.* New York: Crown, 1957. Print.

15. Kenny, Jack. "1960: A Year That Changed America." *The New American.* The New American Magazine, 19 Feb. 2010. Web. <http://www.thenewamerican.com/history/american/2958-1960-a-year-that-changed-america>.

16. Brownell, Richard. *American Counterculture of the 1960s.* Detroit, MI: Lucent, 2011. Print.

17. See #16

18. See #16

19. Sirius, R. U., and Dan Joy. *Counterculture through the Ages: From Abraham to Acid House.* New York: Villard, 2005. Print.

20. Macdonald, Nancy. *The Graffiti Subculture: Youth, Masculinity, and Identity in London and New York.* New York: Palgrave, 2001. Print.

21. Cooper, Ashton. "The Wild and Woolly World of Yarn Bombing, Street Art's Soft Sensation." *Blouin Artinfo.* Louise Blouin Media, 10 June 2011. Web. <http://www.artinfo.com/news/story/37853/the-wild-and-woolly-world-of-yarn-bombing-street-arts-soft-sensation/>.

22. Wollan, Malia. "Graffiti's Cozy, Feminine Side." *The New York Times*. The New York Times Company, 18 May 2011. Web. <http://www.nytimes.com/2011/05/19/fashion/creating-graffiti-with-yarn.html>.

23. Silverman, Julia. "Yarn Bombers Have a Blast in Portland." *OregonLive.com*. Oregon Live LLC, 9 Sept. 2010. Web. <http://www.oregonlive.com/portland/index.ssf/2010/09/yarn_bombers_have_a_blast_in_p.html>.

24. Côté, James E., and Charles Levine. *Identity Formation, Agency, and Culture: A Social Psychological Synthesis*. Mahwah, NJ: L. Erlbaum Associates, 2002. Print.

25. Anderson, Chris. *The Long Tail: Why the Future of Business Is Selling Less of More*. New York: Hyperion, 2006. Print.

26. Carter, Rita. *Multiplicity: The New Science of Personality, Identity, and the Self*. New York: Little, Brown &, 2008. Print.

27. Muggleton, David, and Rupert Weinzierl. *The Post-subcultures Reader*. Oxford: Berg, 2003. Print.

28. Blau, Melinda, and Karen L. Fingerman. *Consequential Strangers: The Power of People Who Don't Seem to Matter-- but Really Do*. New York: W.W. Norton &, 2009. Print.

29. *The Legend of Leigh Bowery*. Dir. Charles Atlas. Perf. Leigh Bowery. Atlas Films, 2002. DVD.

30. "Tattoo Timeline." *New York Guides*. New York Media LLC, 24 Sept. 2007. Web. <http://nymag.com/guides/everything/tattoos/37978/>.

31. Laumann, A., and A. Derick. "Tattoos and Body Piercings in the United States: A National Data Set." *Journal of the American Academy of Dermatology* 55.3 (2006): 413-21. Print.

32. Penn, Mark J., and E. Kinney. Zalesne. *Microtrends: The Small Forces behind Tomorrow's Big Changes*. New York: Twelve, 2007. Print.

33. Mann, Aimee. "Aimee Mann Quote." *Great-Quotes.com*. Great Quotes.com. Web. <http://www.great-quotes.com/quote/26688>.

34. *Easy Rider.* Dir. Dennis Hopper. Perf. Peter Fonda, Dennis Hopper and Jack Nicholson. Columbia Pictures, 1969. DVD.

35. *The Big Lebowski.* Dir. Ethan Coen and Joel Coen. Perf. Jeff Bridges, John Goodman and Julianne Moore. Polygram Filmed Entertainment, 1998. DVD.

36. Captain Jean Luc Picard. "Rule 34." *Urban Dictionary.* Urban Dictionary, 29 Oct. 2006. Web. <http://www.urbandictionary. com/define.php?term=Rule%2034>.

37. Palfrey, John G., and Urs Gasser. *Born Digital: Understanding the First Generation of Digital Natives.* New York: Basic, 2008. Print.

38. EMC Corporation. Amount of Digital Information Created in 2010 to Reach 1.2 Zettabytes. *Photoxels.* Photoxels, 4 May 2010. Web. <http://www.photoxels.com/pr-emc-annual-data-growth/>.

39. See #25

40. See #25

41. Dailey, Kate. "Amit Gupta's Good News: Marrow Donor Finds Match." *BBC News Magazine.* BBC, 19 Jan. 2012. Web. <http:// www.bbc.co.uk/news/magazine-16640491>.

42. The Sherman Brothers. "It's a Small World." *It's a Small World.* 1963. MP3.

43. "It's a Small World." *Disneyland Resort.* Disney. Web. <http:// disneyland.disney.go.com/disneyland/its-a-small-world/?name=its asmallworldAttractionPage>.

44. Gibson, Campbell J., and Emily Lennon. *Historical Census Statistics on the Foreign-born Population of the United States: 1850-1990.* Rep. no. POPULATION DIVISION WORKING PAPER NO. 29. Washington, D.C.: U.S. Bureau of the Census, 1999. Print.

45. Pan, Joann. "Social Media Campaign Finds Tech Entrepreneur a Bone Marrow Donor." Web log post. *Mashable Social Media.* Mashable, Inc., 19 Jan. 2012. Web. <http://mashable. com/2012/01/19/amit-gupta-finds-donor/>.

46. "Dictionaries: The June Issue of the Oxford English Dictionary Newsletter Is Now Online; Google As a Verb Now in Oxford English Dictionary." *Resource Shelf.* Free Pint Limited, 28 June 2006. Web. <http://web.resourceshelf.com/go/resourceblog/42925>.

47. Akhtar, Shabbir. "Facebook To Reach Half Of The U.S. Population In 2013: EMarketer." *Socialtrakr.com.* Socialtrakr, 25 Feb. 2011. Web. <http://www.socialtrakr.com/2011/02/25/facebook-to-reach-half-of-the-u-s-population-in-2013-emarketer/>.

48. Hodkinson, Paul. *Goth: Identity, Style, and Subculture.* Oxford: Berg, 2002. Print.

49. Sharp, John. "Top 10 Statistics on Online Dating." *Man Vs. Date.* 28 Jan. 2011. Web. <http://manvsdate.com/top-10-statistics-online-dating/>.

50. "Match.com Releases Study on Trends in Online Dating." *Match.com.* 30 Apr. 2010. Web. <http://www.datingsitesreviews.com/article.php?story=Match-Releases-Study-Trends-Online-Datin>.

51. Jeremy [jedberg]. "Your Gold Dollars at Work." Web log post. *Blog.reddit.* Reddit, 26 July 2010. Web. <http://blog.reddit.com/2010/07/your-gold-dollars-at-work.html>.

52. *Metareddit.* Web. <http://metareddit.com/>.

53. Hopfensperger, Jean. "Kenyan Tale Shows Power of Online Giving." *StarTribune.* 6 Feb. 2012. Web. <http://www.startribune.com/lifestyle/138617664.html>.

54. "Statistics for Secret Santa 2011." *Reddit Gifts.* Web. <http://redditgifts.com/statistics/secret-santa-2011/>.

55. "Scumbag Steve." *Reddit.* Web. <http://www.reddit.com/r/ScumbagSteve>.

56. Nopooshallpass. "IAmA Guy That Hasn't Pooped in the Month of August Yet. Ask Me Anything about My Extreme Constipation." *Reddit.* 19 Aug. 2011. Web. <http://www.reddit.com/r/IAmA/comments/jo5at/iama_guy_that_hasnt_pooped_in_the_month_of_august/>.

57. Jfallows. "I Am James Fallows, National Correspondent for the Atlantic (and Long-ago Speechwriter for Long-ago President Jimmy Carter) AMA." *Reddit.* 8 Feb. 2012. Web. <http://www.reddit.com/r/IAmA/comments/pged2/i_am_james_fallows_national_correspondent_for_the/>.

58. "SOPA Supporters Before And After." *WeKnowMemes.* WeKnowMemes LLC, 20 Jan. 2012. Web. <http://weknowmemes.com/2012/01/sopa-supporters-before-and-after/>.

59. Grossman, Lev. "You — Yes, You — Are TIME's Person of the Year." *Time Magazine* 25 Dec. 2006. Web. <http://www.time.com/time/magazine/article/0,9171,1570810,00.html>.

60. Gilbert, Daniel Todd. *Stumbling on Happiness.* New York: Vintage, 2007. Print.

61. Gibson, William. "God's Little Toys." *WIRED Magazine* July 2005. Web. <http://www.wired.com/wired/archive/13.07/gibson.html>.

62. "Site Statistics." *Imgur.* Imgur, LLC. Web. <http://imgur.com/stats/month>.

63. Zuckerberg, Mark. "200 Million Strong." Web log post. *The Facebook Blog.* Facebook, 8 Apr. 2009. Web. <http://blog.facebook.com/blog.php?post=72353897130>.

64. "Fact Sheet." *Facebook.* Web. <http://newsroom.fb.com/content/default.aspx?NewsAreaId=22>.

65. Cacioppo, John T., and William Patrick. *Loneliness: Human Nature and the Need for Social Connection.* New York: W.W. Norton &, 2008. Print.

66. Kets, De Vries, Manfred. *Sex, Money, Happiness, and Death: The Quest for Authenticity.* London/Basingstoke: Palgrave Macmillan, 2009. Print.

67. Madden, Mary, and Kathryn Zickuhr. "65% of Online Adults Use Social Networking Sites." *Pew Internet.* Pew Research Center's Internet & American Life Project, 26 Aug. 2011. Web. <http://pewinternet.org/Reports/2011/Social-Networking-Sites.aspx>.

68. Lenhart, Amanda, Mary Madden, Aaron Smith, Kristen Purcell, Kathryn Zickuhr, and Lee Rainie. "Teens, Kindness and Cruelty on Social Network Sites." *Pew Internet.* Pew Research Center's Internet & American Life Project, 9 Nov. 2011. Web. <http://pewinternet. org/Reports/2011/Teens-and-social-media.aspx>.

69. Wilson, David. "More Than Half of Facebook Users Need Their Dose Daily: Chart of the Day." *Bloomberg.* Bloomberg L.P., 2 Feb. 2012. Web. <http://www.bloomberg.com/news/2012-02-03/ facebook-turns-into-daily-habit-for-more-users-chart-of-the-day. html>.

70. Jennydavis. "Theory Meets Methods: Data & the Authentic Cyborg Self." Web log post. *Cyborgology.* The Society Pages, 5 Dec. 2010. Web. <http://thesocietypages.org/cyborgology/2010/12/05/ theory-meets-methods-data-the-authentic-cyborg-self/>.

71. Leland, John. *Hip: The History.* New York, NY: HarperCollins, 2004. Print.

72. See #65

73. See #65

74. Paul, Pamela. "Does Facebook Make Someone Social Offline?" *The New York Times.* The New York Times Company, 28 Jan. 2011, New York ed. The New York Times. 30 Jan. 2011. Web. <http:// www.nytimes.com/2011/01/30/fashion/30Studied.html>.

75. Zax, David. "This Is Your Brain on Facebook." *Fast Company.* Mansueto Ventures, LLC, 2 Mar. 2011. Web. <http://www. fastcompany.com/1733483/this-is-your-brain-on-facebook>.

76. A Tribe Called Quest. "Skypager." *The Low End Theory.* 1991. MP3.

77. Postrel, Virginia I. *The Substance of Style: How the Rise of Aesthetic Value Is Remaking Commerce, Culture, and Consciousness.* New York: HarperCollins, 2003. Print.

78. Conley, Chip. *The Rebel Rules: Daring to Be Yourself in Business.* New York: Simon & Schuster, 2001. Print.

79. Frucci, Adam. "If You Can't Afford a Bugatti Car, Maybe You Can Afford Their Toaster." *Gizmodo.* 12 Sept. 2007. Web. <http://gizmodo.com/299162/if-you-cant-afford-a-bugatti-car-maybe-you-can-afford-their-toaster>.

80. Heath, Joseph, and Andrew Potter. *Nation of Rebels: Why Counterculture Became Consumer Culture.* New York: HarperBusiness, 2004. Print.

81. "Supermarket Facts: Industry Overview 2010." *Food Marketing Institute.* Matrix Group International, Inc. Web. <http://www.fmi.org/facts_figs/?fuseaction=superfact>.

82. Bialik, Carl. "Starbucks Stays Mum on Drink Math." *WSJ Blogs.* The Wall Street Journal, 2 Apr. 2008. Web. <http://blogs.wsj.com/numbersguy/starbucks-stays-mum-on-drink-math-309/1/>.

83. See #32

84. See #25

85. Tapscott, Don. *Grown up Digital: How the Net Generation Is Changing Your World.* New York: McGraw-Hill, 2009. Print.

86. *Steel Magnolias.* Dir. Herbert Ross. Perf. Sally Field, Dolly Parton, Julia Roberts, Daryl Hannah, Olympia Dukakis, Shirley MacLaine, Tom Skerritt, and Sam Shepard. Tri-Star, 1989. DVD.

87. Gelder, Ken. *Subcultures: Cultural Histories and Social Practice.* London: Routledge, 2007. Print.

88. Smith, JR. "Kids Are Learning Computer Skills before Life Skills." Web log post. *View from the Top.* AVG Official Blogs, 19 Jan. 2011. Web. <http://blogs.avg.com/view-from-the-top/kids-learning-computer-skills-before-life-skills/>.

89. Springer Science+Business Media. "Children Now Enjoy More Freedom At Home, But Are More Restricted Outside The Home." *ScienceDaily,* 4 Aug. 2009. Web. 2 Mar. 2012.

90. Rubin, Sylvia. "Invasion of the Teletubbies." *San Francisco Chronicle* 30 Mar. 1998. Web. <http://www.sfgate.com/cgi-bin/article.cgi?f=/c/a/1998/03/30/DD75322.DTL>.

91. "Crazy Toyota Creatures." *Apps4Kids.* 15 Feb. 2012. Web. <http://www.apps4kids.net/2012/02/15/crazy-toyota-creatures/>.

92. Marwick, Alice E., Murgia-Diaz, Diego and Palfrey, John G., *Youth, Privacy and Reputation (Literature Review).* Berkman Center Research Publication No. 2010-5; Harvard Public Law Working Paper No. 10-29. Available at SSRN: http://ssrn.com/abstract=1588163

93. See #92

94. See #37

95. See #92

96. See #92

97. Lenhart, Amanda, Kristen Purcell, Aaron Smith, and Kathryn Zickuhr. "Pew Internet Social Media and Young Adults." *Social Media and Young Adults.* Pew Research Center's Internet & American Life Project, 3 Feb. 2010. Web. <http://pewinternet.org/Reports/2010/Social-Media-and-Young-Adults/Part-3/6-Content-Creation.aspx>.

98. Manafy, Michelle, and Heidi Gautschi. *Dancing with Digital Natives: Staying in Step with the Generation That's Transforming the Way Business Is Done.* Medford, NJ: CyberAge, 2011. Print.

99. See #25

100. See #77

101. See #77

102. U.S. Bureau of Labor Statistics. Division of Labor Force Statistics. *Employee Tenure Summary.* Bureau of Labor Statistics. 14 Sept. 2010. Web. <http://www.bls.gov/news.release/tenure.nr0.htm>.

103. Hansen, Kristin A. "Geographical Mobility." *U.S. Census Bureau.* U.S. Census Bureau, Population Division. Web. <http://www.census.gov/population/www/pop-profile/geomob.html>.

104. Cacioppo, John T., Penny S. Visser, and Cynthia L. Pickett. *Social Neuroscience: People Thinking about Thinking People.* Cambridge, MA: MIT, 2006. Print.

105. Qualman, Erik. "10 WOW Social Media Statistics." *Socialnomics.* 7 June 2011. Web. <http://www.socialnomics.net/2011/06/07/10-wow-social-media-statistics/>.

106. "More than Half of 18-29-Yr-Olds Own Smartphones." *Marketing Charts.* Watershed Publishing, 12 July 2011. Web. <http://www.marketingcharts.com/direct/more-than-half-of-18-29-yr-olds-own-smartphones-18268/>.

107. Pratt, Andrew. "Email Overload in the Workplace: A Multi-Dimensional Exploration." *Orange Journal.* EServer, 9 Jan. 2006. Web. <http://orange.eserver.org/issues/5-1/pratt.html>.

108. Joe. "The History of the BlackBerry." *BB Geeks.* MFE Interactive, 15 Apr. 2008. Web. <http://www.bbgeeks.com/blackberry-guides/the-history-of-the-blackberry-88296/>.

109. Mashable Video. "There Will Be More Smartphones Than Humans on the Planet by Year's End [VIDEO]." Web log post. *Mashable Tech.* Mashable, Inc., 14 Feb. 2012. Web. <http://mashable.com/2012/02/14/more-smartphones-than-humans/>.

110. "2 in 3 Online Adults Use SocNets." *Marketing Charts.* Watershed Publishing, 29 Aug. 2011. Web. <http://www.marketingcharts.com/direct/2-in-3-online-adults-use-socnets-18975/>.

111. "2012 Consumer Privacy Index | Q1." *TRUSTe.* TRUSTe, Inc. Web. <http://www.truste.com/consumer-privacy-index-Q1-2012/>.

112. Krebs, Brian. "Court Rules Against Teacher in MySpace 'Drunken Pirate' Case." *The Washington Post.* The Washington Post, 3 Dec. 2008. Web. <http://voices.washingtonpost.com/securityfix/2008/12/court_rules_against_teacher_in.html>.

113. Constine, Josh. "Pinterest Hits 10 Million U.S. Monthly Uniques Faster Than Any Standalone Site Ever -comScore." Weblog post. *TechCrunch.* AOL Inc., 7 Feb. 2012. Web. <http://techcrunch.com/2012/02/07/pinterest-monthly-uniques/>.

114. See #92

115. Khatib, Firas, Frank DiMaio, Seth Cooper, Maciej Kazmierczyk, Miroslaw Gilski, Szymon Krzywda, Helena Zabranska, Iva Pichova, James Thompson, Zoran Popović, Mariusz Jaskolski, and David Baker. "Crystal Structure of a Monomeric Retroviral Protease Solved by Protein Folding Game Players." *Nature Structural & Molecular Biology* 18.10 (2011): 1175-177. Print.

116. Boyle, Alan. "Gamers Solve Molecular Puzzle That Baffled Scientists." Web log post. *Cosmic Log.* MSNBC.com, 18 Sept. 2011. Web. <http://cosmiclog.msnbc.msn.com/_news/2011/09/18/7802623-gamers-solve-molecular-puzzle-that-baffled-scientists>.

117. Clark, Luke, Andrew J. Lawrence, Frances Astley-Jones, and Nicola Gray. "Gambling Near-Misses Enhance Motivation to Gamble and Recruit Win-Related Brain Circuitry." *Neuron* 61.3 (2009): 481-90. Print.

118. "Gamification." *Wikipedia.* Web. 25 Feb. 2011. <http://en.wikipedia.org/wiki/Gamification>.

119. Ungerleider, Neal. "Wannabe SEALs Help U.S. Navy Hunt Pirates In Massively Multiplayer Game." *Fast Company.* Mansueto Ventures, LLC, 10 May 2011. Web. <http://www.fastcompany.com/1752574/the-us-navys-massively-multiplayer-pirate-hunting-game>.

120. Noyes, Katherine. "Marriott Creates Facebook Game for International Recruitment." *Springwise.* 22 June 2011. Web. <http://www.springwise.com/tourism_travel/marriottgame/>.

121. McRae, Judy. "PepsiCo Launches 'Possibilities' Mobile App for Recruitment." *Springwise.* 26 May 2011. Web. <http://www.springwise.com/marketing_advertising/pepsipossibilities/>.

122. Fawkes, Piers. "Al Gore: Games Are The New Normal." *PSFK.* 2 Dec. 2011. Web. <http://www.psfk.com/2011/12/al-gore-games-are-the-new-normal.html>.

123. Chen, Yi. "How Is Gamification Influencing Mainstream Corporate Culture? [Infographic]." *PSFK.* 10 Jan. 2012. Web. <http://www.psfk.com/2012/01/gamification-mainstream-corporate-culture.html>.

124. Bryner, Jeanna. "Most Students Bored at School." Web log post. *LiveScience*. TechMediaNetwork.com, 28 Feb. 2007. Web. <http://www.livescience.com/1308-students-bored-school.html>.

125. See #85

126. See #85

127. See #85

128. Messick, David M., Roderick M. Kramer, Ann E. Tenbrunsel, and Max H. Bazerman. *Social Decision Making: Social Dilemmas, Social Values, and Ethical Judgments*. New York: Routledge, 2010. Print.

129. Akerlof, George A., and Rachel E. Kranton. *Identity Economics: How Our Identities Shape Our Work, Wages, and Well-being*. Princeton: Princeton UP, 2010. Print.

130. Sawers, Paul. "Home, Sweet Home: 60% of UK Employees Could Be Working Remotely within a Decade." *The Next Web*. 22 Feb. 2012. Web. <http://thenextweb.com/uk/2012/02/22/home-sweet-home-60-of-uk-employees-could-be-working-remotely-within-a-decade/>.

131. Stillman, Jessica. "Scientists Prove Telecommuting Is Awesome." Web log post. *GigaOM*. 14 Nov. 2011. Web. <http://gigaom.com/collaboration/scientists-prove-telecommuting-is-awesome/>.

132. Staples, Inc. There's No Place Like a Home Office: Staples Survey Shows Telecommuters Are Happier and Healthier, With 25% Less Stress When Working from Home. 19 July 2011. Web. <http://staples.newshq.businesswire.com/press-release/corporate/there%E2%80%99s-no-place-home-office-staples-survey-shows-telecommuters-are-happier-#ixzz1UBEqvM86>.

133. Fonner, Kathryn, and Michael Roloff. "Why Teleworkers Are More Satisfied with Their Jobs than Are Office-Based Workers: When Less Contact Is Beneficial." *Journal of Applied Communication Research* 38.4 (2010): 336-61. Print.

134. Carey, Benedict. "Tracing the Spark of Creative Problem-Solving." *The New York Times*. The New York Times Company, 7 Dec. 2010, New York ed. The New York Times. 6 Dec. 2010. Web.

<http://www.nytimes.com/2010/12/07/science/07brain.html>.

135. See #134

136. Doward, Jamie. "Happy People Really Do Work Harder." *The Observer* 10 July 2010. The Guardian. Web. <http://www.guardian. co.uk/science/2010/jul/11/happy-workers-are-more-productive>.

137. University of Michigan. "Friends with cognitive benefits: Mental function improves after certain kinds of socializing." *ScienceDaily,* 28 Oct. 2010. Web. <http://www.sciencedaily.com/ releases/2010/10/101028113817.htm>.

138. Sanders, Tim. *The Likeability Factor: How to Boost Your L-factor & Achieve Your Life's Dreams.* New York: Crown, 2005. Print.

139. Fahmy, Miral. "Facebook, YouTube at Work Make Better Employees: Study." *Reuters Life!* Ed. Valerie Lee. Reuters, 2 Apr. 2009. Web. <http://www.reuters.com/article/2009/04/02/us-work-internet-idUSTRE5310ZH20090402>.

140. Academy of Management. Internet Browsing at Work? It's a Pause That Refreshes Workers and Enhances Their Productivity, New Research Finds. *Academy of Management.* Pace University, Aug. 2011. Web. <http://www.aomonline.org/aom.asp?ID=251&page_ ID=224&pr_id=448>.

141. Hsu, Tiffany. "Best Study Ever: Wasting Time Online Boosts Worker Productivity." *Los Angeles Times.* Los Angeles Times, 17 Aug. 2011. Web. <http://latimesblogs.latimes.com/money_co/2011/08/ best-study-ever-wasting-time-online-boosts-productivity-at-work. html>.

142. See #85

143. "Google Trends: Hipster." *Google.* Web. 11 Apr. 2012. <http:// www.google.com/trends/?q=hipster&ctab=0&geo=all&date=all& sort=0>.

INFOGRAPHIC CITATIONS

CONTENT, CONTENT EVERYWHERE (CHAPTER 2.1)

a. Schmidt, Eric. "Technology Is Making Marketing Accountable." Speech. *Google*. Association of National Advertisers, 8 Oct. 2005. Web. <http://www.google.com/press/podium/ana.html>.

    Birge, Robert. "Human Brain." *Sizes*. Sizes, Inc., 20 Sept. 2007. Web. <http://www.sizes.com/people/brain.htm>.

b. Radicati, Sara. *Email Statistics Report, 2010-2014*. Rep. The Radicati Group, Inc., 19 Apr. 2010. Web. <http://www.radicati.com/?p=5290>.

    "Google Queries per Second." *Wolfram Alpha*. Wolfram Alpha LLC. Web. 5 Mar. 2012. <http://www.wolframalpha.com/input/?i=google+queries+per+second>.

    "Statistics." *YouTube*. YouTube, LLC. Web. 5 Mar. 2012. <http://www.youtube.com/t/press_statistics>.

    One Minute on Facebook. Time Video. Time Inc. Web. 5 Mar. 2012. <http://www.time.com/time/video/player/0,32068,711054024001_2037229,00.html>

c. Anderson, Chris. *The Long Tail: Why the Future of Business Is Selling Less of More*. New York: Hyperion, 2006. Print.

OUR GLOBAL NEIGHBORS
(CHAPTER 2.2)

a.   Gibson, Campbell J., and Emily Lennon. *Historical Census Statistics on the Foreign-born Population of the United States: 1850-1990.* Rep. no. Population Division Working Paper No. 29. Washington, D.C.: U.S. Bureau of the Census, 1999. Print.

b.   "12 Percent in U.S. Foreign Born." *UPI.com.* United Press International, Inc., 19 Oct. 2010. Web. <http://www.upi.com/Top_News/US/2010/10/19/12-percent-in-US-foreign-born/UPI-87261287522622/>.

c.   Skinner, Curtis, Vanessa R. Wight, Yumiko Aratani, Janice L. Cooper, and Kalyani Thampi. *English Language Proficiency, Family Economic Security, and Child Development.* Publication. National Center for Children in Poverty, June 2010. Web. <http://www.nccp.org/publications/pub_948.html>.

d.   Hobbs, Frank and Nicole Stoops, U.S. Census Bureau, Census 2000 Special Reports, Series CENSR-4, *Demographic Trends in the 20th Century,* U.S. Government Printing Office, Washington, DC, 2002

e, f.   Easterbrook, Gregg. *The Progress Paradox: How Life Gets Better While People Feel Worse.* New York: Random House, 2003. Print.

g.   Heron MP, Hoyert DL, Xu J, Scott C, Tejada-Vera B. *Deaths: Preliminary data for 2006.* National vital statistics reports; vol 56 no 16. Hyattsville, MD: National Center for Health Statistics. 2008

     National Center for Health Statistics, *National Vital Statistics Reports.* Web:www.cdc.gov/nchs.

BABY'S FIRST INTERNET (CHAPTER 3.3)

a. Smith, JR. *"Would You Want a Digital Footprint from Birth?"* Web log post. View from the Top. AVG Official Blogs, 6 Oct. 2010. Web. <http://blogs.avg.com/view-from-the-top/would-you-want-a-digital-footprint-from-birth/>.

b. Smith, JR. *"Kids Are Learning Computer Skills before Life Skills."* Web log post. View from the Top. AVG Official Blogs, 19 Jan. 2011. Web. <http://blogs.avg.com/view-from-the-top/kids-learning-computer-skills-before-life-skills/>.

c. Blackshaw, Pete. *"A Pocket Guide to Social Media and Kids."* Web log post. Nielsen Wire. Nielsen, 2 Nov. 2009. Web. <http://blog.nielsen.com/nielsenwire/consumer/a-pocket-guide-to-social-media-and-kids/>.

d. Orenstein, Peggy. *"Why Parents Lie to Let Kids Join Facebook."* Web log post. The New York Times: Motherlode. The New York Times Company, 3 Nov. 2011. Web. <http://parenting.blogs.nytimes.com/2011/11/03/why-parents-lie-to-let-kids-join-facebook/>.

LIFE. MEET WORK. WORK. MEET LIFE. (CHAPTER 4.1)

a. "Doing Business in Bed, When Sick & on Vacation." *Clean Cut Media.* 23 Sept. 2010. Web. <http://www.cleancutmedia.com/news/emailing-in-bed-when-sick-on-vacation>.

b, c. Fox, Zoe. "Shocker: Most Americans Check Work Email During Holidays." *Mashable Business.* Mashable, Inc., 28 Nov. 2011. Web. <http://mashable.com/2011/11/28/email-work-holiday/>.

d. Moore, Brian J. "Social Networking in the Workplace." *National Law Review.* Dinsmore & Shohl LLP, 19 Oct. 2011. Web. <http://www.natlawreview.com/article/social-networking-workplace>.

e. "Gen Y Facebook Users Seen Mixing Business With Pleasure." *Marketing Charts.* Watershed Publishing, 9 Jan. 2012. Web. <http://www.marketingcharts.com/direct/gen-y-facebook-users-seen-mixing-business-with-pleasure-20698/>.

f. Eler, Alicia. "91% Of Hiring Mangers [sic] Use Social Networking To Screen."*ReadWriteWeb.* ReadWriteWeb, 5 Oct. 2011. Web. <http://www.readwriteweb.com/archives/91_of_hiring_mangers_use_social_networking_to_scre.php>.

g. Rosen, Jeffrey. "The Web Means the End of Forgetting." *The New York Times.* The New York Times Company, 21 July 2010. Web. <http://www.nytimes.com/2010/07/25/magazine/25privacy-t2.html>.

BIBLIOGRAPHY

"12 Percent in U.S. Foreign Born." *UPI.com*. United Press International, Inc., 19 Oct. 2010. Web. <http://www.upi.com/ Top_News/US/2010/10/19/12-percent-in-US-foreign-born/UPI-87261287522622/>.

"2 in 3 Online Adults Use SocNets." *Marketing Charts*. Watershed Publishing, 29 Aug. 2011. Web. <http://www.marketingcharts.com/ direct/2-in-3-online-adults-use-socnets-18975/>.

"2012 Consumer Privacy Index | Q1." *TRUSTe*. TRUSTe, Inc. Web. <http://www.truste.com/consumer-privacy-index-Q1-2012/>.

"Crazy Toyota Creatures." *Apps4Kids*. 15 Feb. 2012. Web. <http://www. apps4kids.net/2012/02/15/crazy-toyota-creatures/>.

"Dictionaries: The June Issue of the Oxford English Dictionary Newsletter Is Now Online; Google As a Verb Now in Oxford English Dictionary." *Resource Shelf*. Free Pint Limited, 28 June 2006. Web. <http://web.resourceshelf.com/go/resourceblog/42925>.

"Doing Business in Bed, When Sick & on Vacation." *Clean Cut Media*. 23 Sept. 2010. Web. <http://www.cleancutmedia.com/news/emailing-in-bed-when-sick-on-vacation>.

"Fact Sheet." *Facebook*. Web. <http://newsroom.fb.com/content/default. aspx?NewsAreaId=22>.

"Gamification." *Wikipedia*. Web. 25 Feb. 2011. <http://en.wikipedia. org/wiki/Gamification>.

"Gen Y Facebook Users Seen Mixing Business With Pleasure." *Marketing Charts*. Watershed Publishing, 9 Jan. 2012. Web. <http://www. marketingcharts.com/direct/gen-y-facebook-users-seen-mixing-business-with-pleasure-20698/>.

"Google Queries per Second." *Wolfram Alpha.* Wolfram Alpha LLC. Web. 5 Mar. 2012. <http://www.wolframalpha.com/input/?i=google+queries+per+second>.

"Google Trends: Hipster." *Google.* Web. 30 Sept. 2011. <http://www.google.com/trends/?q=hipster&ctab=0&geo=all&date=all&sort=0>.

"Hardly Working – A Look into Business at the Workplace." *Online MBA.* 22 Nov. 2010. Web. <http://www.onlinemba.com/blog/hardly-working-a-look-into-business-at-the-workplace/>.

"Hipster." *Cracked.com.* Demand Media, Inc. Web. <http://www.cracked.com/funny-4573-hipster/>.

"It's a Small World." *Disneyland Resort.* Disney. Web. <http://disneyland.disney.go.com/disneyland/its-a-small-world/?name=itsasmallworldAttractionPage>.

"Match.com Releases Study on Trends in Online Dating." *Match.com.* 30 Apr. 2010. Web. <http://www.datingsitesreviews.com/article.php?story=Match-Releases-Study-Trends-Online-Datin>.

"Meet the Global Scenester: He's Hip. He's Cool. He's Everywhere." *The Independent.* 14 Aug. 2008. Web. <http://www.independent.co.uk/life-style/fashion/features/meet-the-global-scenester-hes-hip-hes-cool-hes-everywhere-894199.html>.

"More than Half of 18-29-Yr-Olds Own Smartphones." *Marketing Charts.* Watershed Publishing, 12 July 2011. Web. <http://www.marketingcharts.com/direct/more-than-half-of-18-29-yr-olds-own-smartphones-18268/>.

"Scumbag Steve." *Reddit.* Web. <http://www.reddit.com/r/ScumbagSteve>.

"Site Statistics." *Imgur.* Imgur, LLC. Web. <http://imgur.com/stats/month>.

"SOPA Supporters Before And After." *WeKnowMemes.* WeKnowMemes LLC, 20 Jan. 2012. Web. <http://weknowmemes.com/2012/01/sopa-supporters-before-and-after/>.

"Statistics for Secret Santa 2011." *Reddit Gifts.* Web. <http://redditgifts.com/statistics/secret-santa-2011/>.

"Statistics." *YouTube*. YouTube, LLC. Web. 5 Mar. 2012. <http://www.youtube.com/t/press_statistics>.

"Supermarket Facts: Industry Overview 2010." *Food Marketing Institute*. Matrix Group International, Inc. Web. <http://www.fmi.org/facts_figs/?fuseaction=superfact>.

"Tattoo Timeline." *New York Guides*. New York Media LLC, 24 Sept. 2007. Web. <http://nymag.com/guides/everything/tattoos/37978/>.

"The History of Social Networking." *Online Schools*. 2010. Web. <http://www.onlineschools.org/blog/history-of-social-networking/>.

"Why the Hipster Must Die: The Hipsterati Talks Back." *Time Out New York* 29 May 2007. Web. <http://newyork.timeout.com/things-to-do/this-week-in-new-york/8364/why-the-hipster-must-die-the-hipsterati-talks-back>.

A Tribe Called Quest. "Skypager." *The Low End Theory*. 1991. MP3.

Academy of Management. Internet Browsing at Work? It's a Pause That Refreshes Workers and Enhances Their Productivity, New Research Finds. *Academy of Management*. Pace University, Aug. 2011. Web. <http://www.aomonline.org/aom.asp?ID=251&page_ID=224&pr_id=448>.

Akerlof, George A., and Rachel E. Kranton. *Identity Economics: How Our Identities Shape Our Work, Wages, and Well-being*. Princeton: Princeton UP, 2010. Print.

Akhtar, Shabbir. "Facebook To Reach Half Of The U.S. Population In 2013: EMarketer." *Socialtrakr.com*. Socialtrakr, 25 Feb. 2011. Web. <http://www.socialtrakr.com/2011/02/25/facebook-to-reach-half-of-the-u-s-population-in-2013-emarketer/>.

Anderson, Chris. *The Long Tail: Why the Future of Business Is Selling Less of More*. New York: Hyperion, 2006. Print.

Anderson, Jon. "Prohibition Was Never This Funny." *Chicago Tribune* 23 Sept. 1985. Print.

Baron, Naomi S. *Always On: Language in an Online and Mobile World*. Oxford: Oxford UP, 2008. Print.

Bialik, Carl. "Starbucks Stays Mum on Drink Math." *WSJ Blogs.* The Wall Street Journal, 2 Apr. 2008. Web. <http://blogs.wsj.com/numbersguy/starbucks-stays-mum-on-drink-math-309/1/>.

Birge, Robert. "Human Brain." *Sizes.* Sizes, Inc., 20 Sept. 2007. Web. <http://www.sizes.com/people/brain.htm>.

Blackshaw, Pete. "A Pocket Guide to Social Media and Kids." Web log post. *Nielsen Wire.* Nielsen, 2 Nov. 2009. Web. <http://blog.nielsen.com/nielsenwire/consumer/a-pocket-guide-to-social-media-and-kids/>.

Blau, Melinda, and Karen L. Fingerman. *Consequential Strangers: The Power of People Who Don't Seem to Matter-- but Really Do.* New York: W.W. Norton &, 2009. Print.

Blossom, John. *Content Nation: Surviving and Thriving as Social Media Changes Our Work, Our Lives, and Our Future.* Indianapolis, IN: Wiley Technology Pub., 2009. Print.

Borow, Zev. "Will The Last Hipster Please Turn Out The Lights?" *New York Guides.* New York Magazine, 21 May 2005. Web. <http://nymag.com/nymetro/urban/features/10488/>.

Boyle, Alan. "Gamers Solve Molecular Puzzle That Baffled Scientists." Web log post. *Cosmic Log.* MSNBC.com, 18 Sept. 2011. Web. <http://cosmiclog.msnbc.msn.com/_news/2011/09/18/7802623-gamers-solve-molecular-puzzle-that-baffled-scientists>.

Branaman, Ann. *Self and Society.* Malden, MA: Blackwell, 2001. Print.

Brenner, Bill. "6 Ways We Gave Up Our Privacy." *CSO.* CXO Media Inc., 12 Oct. 2009. Web. <http://www.csoonline.com/article/504793/6-ways-we-gave-up-our-privacy>.

Brownell, Richard. *American Counterculture of the 1960s.* Detroit, MI: Lucent, 2011. Print.

Bryner, Jeanna. "Most Students Bored at School." Web log post. *LiveScience.* TechMediaNetwork.com, 28 Feb. 2007. Web. <http://www.livescience.com/1308-students-bored-school.html>.

Burns, Peter, and Marina Novelli. *Tourism and Social Identities: Global Frameworks and Local Realities.* Amsterdam: Elsevier, 2006. Print.

Bustillos, Maria. "Wikipedia And The Death Of The Expert." *The Awl.* 17 May 2011. Web. <http://www.theawl.com/2011/05/wikipedia-and-the-death-of-the-expert>.

Cacioppo, John T. *Foundations in Social Neuroscience.* Cambridge, MA: MIT, 2002. Print.

Cacioppo, John T., and William Patrick. *Loneliness: Human Nature and the Need for Social Connection.* New York: W.W. Norton &, 2008. Print.

Cacioppo, John T., Penny S. Visser, and Cynthia L. Pickett. *Social Neuroscience: People Thinking about Thinking People.* Cambridge, MA: MIT, 2006. Print.

Captain Jean Luc Picard. "Rule 34." *Urban Dictionary.* Urban Dictionary, 29 Oct. 2006. Web. <http://www.urbandictionary.com/define.php?term=Rule%2034>.

Carey, Benedict. "Tracing the Spark of Creative Problem-Solving." *The New York Times.* The New York Times Company, 7 Dec. 2010, New York ed. The New York Times. 6 Dec. 2010. Web. <http://www.nytimes.com/2010/12/07/science/07brain.html>.

Carter, Rita. *Multiplicity: The New Science of Personality, Identity, and the Self.* New York: Little, Brown &, 2008. Print.

Chen, Adrian. "The Online Reputation Gap." *Gawker.* 3 Apr. 2011. Web. <http://gawker.com/5788434/the-coming-online-reputation-gap>.

Chen, Yi. "How Is Gamification Influencing Mainstream Corporate Culture? [Infographic]." *PSFK.* 10 Jan. 2012. Web. <http://www.psfk.com/2012/01/gamification-mainstream-corporate-culture.html>.

Clark, Luke, Andrew J. Lawrence, Frances Astley-Jones, and Nicola Gray. "Gambling Near-Misses Enhance Motivation to Gamble and Recruit Win-Related Brain Circuitry." *Neuron* 61.3 (2009): 481-90. Print.

Conley, Chip. *The Rebel Rules: Daring to Be Yourself in Business.* New York: Simon & Schuster, 2001. Print.

Constine, Josh. "Pinterest Hits 10 Million U.S. Monthly Uniques Faster Than Any Standalone Site Ever -comScore." Weblog post. *TechCrunch.* AOL Inc., 7 Feb. 2012. Web. <http://techcrunch.com/2012/02/07/pinterest-monthly-uniques/>.

Cooper, Ashton. "The Wild and Woolly World of Yarn Bombing, Street Art's Soft Sensation." *Blouin Artinfo*. Louise Blouin Media, 10 June 2011. Web. <http://www.artinfo.com/news/story/37853/the-wild-and-woolly-world-of-yarn-bombing-street-arts-soft-sensation/>.

Côté, James E., and Charles Levine. *Identity Formation, Agency, and Culture: A Social Psychological Synthesis*. Mahwah, NJ: L. Erlbaum Associates, 2002. Print.

Crouch, Andy. "Ten Most Significant Cultural Trends of the Last Decade." *Qideas.org*. Q, 2011. Web. <http://www.qideas.org/blog/ten-most-significant-cultural-trends-of-the-last-decade.aspx>.

Da Silva, Kerry. "Why Hipsters Suck." *Hybrid Magazine*. Sept. 2002. Web. <http://www.hybridmagazine.com/culture/0902/dasilva.shtml>.

Dailey, Kate. "Amit Gupta's Good News: Marrow Donor Finds Match." *BBC News Magazine*. BBC, 19 Jan. 2012. Web. <http://www.bbc.co.uk/news/magazine-16640491>.

DeGrazia, David. *Human Identity and Bioethics*. Cambridge: Cambridge UP, 2005. Print.

Distin, Kate. *Cultural Evolution*. Cambridge [U.K.: Cambridge UP, 2011. Print.

Doward, Jamie. "Happy People Really Do Work Harder." *The Observer* 10 July 2010. The Guardian. Web. <http://www.guardian.co.uk/science/2010/jul/11/happy-workers-are-more-productive>.

Easy Rider. Dir. Dennis Hopper. Perf. Peter Fonda, Dennis Hopper and Jack Nicholson. Columbia Pictures, 1969. DVD.

Eler, Alicia. "91% Of Hiring Mangers [sic] Use Social Networking To Screen."*ReadWriteWeb*. ReadWriteWeb, 5 Oct. 2011. Web. <http://www.readwriteweb.com/archives/91_of_hiring_mangers_use_social_networking_to_scre.php>.

EMC Corporation. Amount of Digital Information Created in 2010 to Reach 1.2 Zettabytes. *Photoxels*. Photoxels, 4 May 2010. Web. <http://www.photoxels.com/pr-emc-annual-data-growth/>.

Fahmy, Miral. "Facebook, YouTube at Work Make Better Employees: Study." *Reuters Life!* Ed. Valerie Lee. Reuters, 2 Apr. 2009. Web.

<http://www.reuters.com/article/2009/04/02/us-work-internet-idUSTRE5310ZH20090402>.

Fake, Caterina. "FOMO and Social Media." Web log post. *Caterina.net.* 15 Mar. 2011. Web. <http://caterina.net/wp-archives/71>.

Fawkes, Piers. "Al Gore: Games Are The New Normal." *PSFK.* 2 Dec. 2011. Web. <http://www.psfk.com/2011/12/al-gore-games-are-the-new-normal.html>.

Feezell, Eric. "Do You Have Hipsters?" *The Morning News.* The Morning News LLC, 21 Apr. 2006. Web. <http://www.themorningnews.org/article/do-you-have-hipsters>.

Fincher, Jonathan. "Trends In 2011: Apps For Kids." *PSFK.* 25 Mar. 2011. Web. <http://www.psfk.com/2011/03/trends-in-2011-apps-for-kids.html>.

Fletcher, Dan. "Hipsters." *Time Magazine* 29 July 2009. Web. <http://www.time.com/time/arts/article/0,8599,1913220,00.html>.

Fonner, Kathryn, and Michael Roloff. "Why Teleworkers Are More Satisfied with Their Jobs than Are Office-Based Workers: When Less Contact Is Beneficial." *Journal of Applied Communication Research* 38.4 (2010): 336-61. Print.

Fox, Zoe. "Shocker: Most Americans Check Work Email During Holidays." *Mashable Business.* Mashable, Inc., 28 Nov. 2011. Web. <http://mashable.com/2011/11/28/email-work-holiday/>.

Frank, Cyrille. "The Race for Attention Is Making Our Society More and More Egotistical." *Owni.eu.* 25 Jan. 2011. Web. <http://owni.eu/2011/01/25/the-race-for-attention-is-making-our-society-more-and-more-egotistical/>.

Freeman, Emily. "Preteen Uses of Facebook Worry Parents." *News Observer.* The News & Observer Publishing Company, 7 Mar. 2011. Web. <http://www.newsobserver.com/2011/03/07/1034547/preteen-uses-of-facebook-worry.html>.

Frucci, Adam. "If You Can't Afford a Bugatti Car, Maybe You Can Afford Their Toaster." *Gizmodo.* 12 Sept. 2007. Web. <http://gizmodo.com/299162/if-you-cant-afford-a-bugatti-car-maybe-you-can-afford-their-toaster>.

Gelder, Ken. *Subcultures: Cultural Histories and Social Practice.* London: Routledge, 2007. Print.

Gibson, Campbell J., and Emily Lennon. Historical *Census Statistics on the Foreign-born Population of the United States: 1850-1990.* Rep. no. Population Division Working Paper No. 29. Washington, D.C.: U.S. Bureau of the Census, 1999. Print.

Gibson, William. "God's Little Toys." *WIRED Magazine* July 2005. Web. <http://www.wired.com/wired/archive/13.07/gibson.html>.

Gilbert, Daniel Todd. *Stumbling on Happiness.* New York: Vintage, 2007. Print.

Gladwell, Malcolm. "The Coolhunt." *The New Yorker* 17 Mar. 1997. Print.

Goffman, Erving. *The Presentation of Self in Everyday Life.* Garden City, NY: Doubleday, 1959. Print.

Goleman, Daniel. *Social Intelligence: The New Science of Human Relationships.* New York: Bantam, 2006. Print.

Golijan, Rosa. "What Happens on the Internet Every 60 Seconds." *Technolog.* MSNBC, 16 June 2011. Web. <http://technolog.msnbc. msn.com/_news/2011/06/16/6874191-what-happens-on-the-internet-every-60-seconds>.

Greif, Mark. "The Hipster in the Mirror." *The New York Times.* The New York Times Company, 12 Nov. 2010. Web. <http://www.nytimes. com/2010/11/14/books/review/Greif-t.html>.

Greif, Mark. "What Was the Hipster?" *New York News & Features.* New York Magazine, 24 Oct. 2010. Web. <http://nymag.com/news/ features/69129/>.

Grossman, Lev. "You — Yes, You — Are TIME's Person of the Year." *Time Magazine* 25 Dec. 2006. Web. <http://www.time.com/time/ magazine/article/0,9171,1570810,00.html>.

Haddow, Douglas. "Hipster: The Dead End of Western Civilization." *Adbusters* 29 July 2008. Web. <http://www.adbusters.org/magazine/79/ hipster.html>.

Hansen, Kristin A. "Geographical Mobility." *U.S. Census Bureau.* U.S.

Census Bureau, Population Division. Web. <http://www.census.gov/population/www/pop-profile/geomob.html>.

Hardaway, Francine. "Don't Look Now, but Your Social Relationships Have Changed--Again." Web log post. *FC Expert.* Fast Company. Mansueto Ventures, LLC. 15 Nov. 2010. Web. <http://www.fastcompany.com/1702776/dont-look-now-but-your-social-relationships-have-changed-again>.

Heath, Joseph, and Andrew Potter. *Nation of Rebels: Why Counterculture Became Consumer Culture.* New York: HarperBusiness, 2004. Print.

Heffel, Lesley. "How Many Hipsters Does It Take to Secede from Brooklyn?" Web log post. *Brooklyn Skeptic.* 5 July 2007. Web. <http://brooklynskeptic.wordpress.com/2007/07/05/how-many-hipsters-does-it-take-to-secede-from-brooklyn/>.

Heron MP, Hoyert DL, Xu J, Scott C, Tejada-Vera B. Deaths: Preliminary data for 2006. *National vital statistics reports*; vol 56 no 16. Hyattsville, MD: National Center for Health Statistics. 2008

Hobbs, Frank and Nicole Stoops, U.S. Census Bureau, Census 2000 Special Reports, Series CENSR-4, *Demographic Trends in the 20th Century,* U.S. Government Printing Office, Washington, DC, 2002

Hodkinson, Paul. *Goth: Identity, Style, and Subculture.* Oxford: Berg, 2002. Print.

Hopfensperger, Jean. "Kenyan Tale Shows Power of Online Giving." *StarTribune.* 6 Feb. 2012. Web. <http://www.startribune.com/lifestyle/138617664.html>.

Horning, Rob. "The Death of the Hipster." *PopMatters.* PopMatters Media, Inc., 13 Apr. 2009. Web. <http://www.popmatters.com/pm/post/the-death-of-the-hipster-panel/>.

Hsu, Tiffany. "Best Study Ever: Wasting Time Online Boosts Worker Productivity." *Los Angeles Times.* Los Angeles Times, 17 Aug. 2011. Web. <http://latimesblogs.latimes.com/money_co/2011/08/best-study-ever-wasting-time-online-boosts-productivity-at-work.html>.

Idan. "Stalking the Wild Hipster." *Everything2.* Everything2 Media, LLC, 9 Nov. 2004. Web. <http://everything2.com/title/Stalking+the+Wild+Hipster>.

Jarvis, Jeff. "One Identity or More?" Web log post. *BuzzMachine*. 8 Mar. 2011. Web. <http://www.buzzmachine.com/2011/03/08/one-identity-or-more/>.

Jenkins, Richard. *Social Identity*. 3rd ed. London: Routledge, 2008. Print.

Jennydavis. "Theory Meets Methods: Data & the Authentic Cyborg Self." Web log post. *Cyborgology*. The Society Pages, 5 Dec. 2010. Web. <http://thesocietypages.org/cyborgology/2010/12/05/theory-meets-methods-data-the-authentic-cyborg-self/>.

Jeremy [jedberg]. "Your Gold Dollars at Work." Web log post. *Blog. reddit*. Reddit, 26 July 2010. Web. <http://blog.reddit.com/2010/07/your-gold-dollars-at-work.html>.

Jfallows. "I Am James Fallows, National Correspondent for the Atlantic (and Long-ago Speechwriter for Long-ago President Jimmy Carter) AMA." *Reddit*. 8 Feb. 2012. Web. <http://www.reddit.com/r/IAmA/comments/pged2/i_am_james_fallows_national_correspondent_for_the/>.

Joe. "The History of the BlackBerry." *BB Geeks*. MFE Interactive, 15 Apr. 2008. Web. <http://www.bbgeeks.com/blackberry-guides/the-history-of-the-blackberry-88296/>.

Johnson, Steven. *Everything Bad Is Good for You: How Today's Popular Culture Is Actually Making Us Smarter*. New York: Riverhead, 2005. Print.

Kenny, Jack. "1960: A Year That Changed America." *The New American*. The New American Magazine, 19 Feb. 2010. Web. <http://www.thenewamerican.com/history/american/2958-1960-a-year-that-changed-america>.

Kephart, William M., and William W. Zellner. *Extraordinary Groups: An Examination of Unconventional Life-styles*. 4th ed. New York: St. Martin's, 1991. Print.

Kets, De Vries, Manfred. *Sex, Money, Happiness, and Death: The Quest for Authenticity*. London/Basingstoke: Palgrave Macmillan, 2009. Print.

Khatib, Firas, Frank DiMaio, Seth Cooper, Maciej Kazmierczyk, Miroslaw Gilski, Szymon Krzywda, Helena Zabranska, Iva Pichova,

James Thompson, Zoran Popović, Mariusz Jaskolski, and David Baker. "Crystal Structure of a Monomeric Retroviral Protease Solved by Protein Folding Game Players." *Nature Structural & Molecular Biology* 18.10 (2011): 1175-177. Print.

Krebs, Brian. "Court Rules Against Teacher in MySpace 'Drunken Pirate' Case." *The Washington Post.* The Washington Post, 3 Dec. 2008. Web. <http://voices.washingtonpost.com/securityfix/2008/12/court_rules_against_teacher_in.html>.

Kurtz, Michael L. *The Challenging of America, 1920-1945.* Arlington Heights, IL: Forum, 1986. Print.

Kyvig, David E. *Daily Life in the United States, 1920-1940: How Americans Lived through the "Roaring Twenties" and the Great Depression.* Chicago: Ivan R. Dee, 2004. Print.

Lanham, Robert. "Look at This F***ing Hipster Basher." *The Morning News.* The Morning News LLC, 29 June 2009. Web. <http://www.themorningnews.org/article/look-at-this-fucking-hipster-basher>.

Laumann, A., and A. Derick. "Tattoos and Body Piercings in the United States: A National Data Set." *Journal of the American Academy of Dermatology* 55.3 (2006): 413-21. Print.

Leach, Anna. "Hipsters Are Agents of Social Change." *The Guardian.* Guardian News and Media Limited, 21 Jan. 2011. Web. <http://www.guardian.co.uk/commentisfree/2011/jan/21/hipsters-gay-people>.

Leland, John. *Hip: The History.* New York, NY: HarperCollins, 2004. Print.

Lenhart, Amanda, Kristen Purcell, Aaron Smith, and Kathryn Zickuhr. "Pew Internet Social Media and Young Adults." *Social Media and Young Adults.* Pew Research Center's Internet & American Life Project, 3 Feb. 2010. Web. <http://pewinternet.org/Reports/2010/Social-Media-and-Young-Adults/Part-3/6-Content-Creation.aspx>.

Lenhart, Amanda, Mary Madden, Aaron Smith, Kristen Purcell, Kathryn Zickuhr, and Lee Rainie. "Teens, Kindness and Cruelty on Social Network Sites." *Pew Internet.* Pew Research Center's Internet & American Life Project, 9 Nov. 2011. Web. <http://pewinternet.org/Reports/2011/Teens-and-social-media.aspx>.

Lorentzen, Christian. "Why the Hipster Must Die." *Time Out* New York 29 May 2007. Web. <http://newyork.timeout.com/things-to-do/this-week-in-new-york/8355/why-the-hipster-must-die>.

Mac, Amber. "5 Tips To Separate Personal And Professional Life Online." *Fast Company.* Mansueto Ventures, LLC. 20 May 2011. Web. <http://www.fastcompany.com/1754431/5-tips-to-separate-personal-professional-life-online>.

Macdonald, Nancy. *The Graffiti Subculture: Youth, Masculinity, and Identity in London and New York.* New York: Palgrave, 2001. Print.

Madden, Mary, and Kathryn Zickuhr. "65% of Online Adults Use Social Networking Sites." *Pew Internet.* Pew Research Center's Internet & American Life Project, 26 Aug. 2011. Web. <http://pewinternet.org/Reports/2011/Social-Networking-Sites.aspx>.

Manafy, Michelle, and Heidi Gautschi. *Dancing with Digital Natives: Staying in Step with the Generation That's Transforming the Way Business Is Done.* Medford, NJ: CyberAge, 2011. Print.

Mann, Aimee. "Aimee Mann Quote." *Great-Quotes.com.* Great Quotes. com. Web. <http://www.great-quotes.com/quote/26688>.

Marwick, Alice E., Murgia-Diaz, Diego and Palfrey, John G., *Youth, Privacy and Reputation (Literature Review).* Berkman Center Research Publication No. 2010-5; Harvard Public Law Working Paper No. 10-29. Available at SSRN: http://ssrn.com/abstract=1588163

Mashable Video. "There Will Be More Smartphones Than Humans on the Planet by Year's End [VIDEO]." Web log post. *Mashable Tech.* Mashable, Inc., 14 Feb. 2012. Web. <http://mashable.com/2012/02/14/more-smartphones-than-humans/>.

McRae, Judy. "PepsiCo Launches 'Possibilities' Mobile App for Recruitment." *Springwise.* 26 May 2011. Web. <http://www.springwise.com/marketing_advertising/pepsipossibilities/>.

Messick, David M., Roderick M. Kramer, Ann E. Tenbrunsel, and Max H. Bazerman. *Social Decision Making: Social Dilemmas, Social Values, and Ethical Judgments.* New York: Routledge, 2010. Print.

Metareddit. Web. <http://metareddit.com/>.

Miller, Claire C. "The Many Faces of You." *The New York Times.* The New York Times Company 17 Oct. 2010, New York ed. Print.

Monaghan, Dave. "In Defense of Hipsters." *Toward Freedom.* 10 Sept. 2008. Web. <http://towardfreedom.com/home/content/view/1404/1/>.

Moore, Brian J. "Social Networking in the Workplace." *National Law Review.* Dinsmore & Shohl LLP, 19 Oct. 2011. Web. <http://www.natlawreview.com/article/social-networking-workplace>.

Moss, J. Jennings. "Dude, "Hipster" Is So 2008." Web log post. *Portfolio.com.* American City Business Journals, 13 Jan. 2011. Web. <http://www.portfolio.com/views/blogs/entrepreneurship/2011/01/13/san-francisco-startup-names-itself-hipster/>.

Muggleton, David, and Rupert Weinzierl. *The Post-subcultures Reader.* Oxford: Berg, 2003. Print.

Nagle, Sarah. "Four Keys To Creating Products For The Lady Gaga Generation." *Fast Company's Co.Design.* Mansueto Ventures, LLC, 1 June 2011. Web. <http://www.fastcodesign.com/1663954/four-keys-to-creating-products-for-the-lady-gaga-generation>.

National Center for Health Statistics, National Vital Statistics Reports. Web:www.cdc.gov/nchs.

Naughton, John. "Personal Privacy Is a Thing of the Past, so You'd Better Get Used to It." *The Observer.* Guardian News and Media Limited, 23 Apr. 2011. Web. <http://www.guardian.co.uk/commentisfree/2011/apr/24/john-naughton-personal-privacy-mobile-phones>.

Nopooshallpass. "IAmA Guy That Hasn't Pooped in the Month of August Yet. Ask Me Anything about My Extreme Constipation." *Reddit.* 19 Aug. 2011. Web. <http://www.reddit.com/r/IAmA/comments/jo5at/iama_guy_that_hasnt_pooped_in_the_month_of_august/>.

Noyes, Katherine. "Marriott Creates Facebook Game for International Recruitment." *Springwise.* 22 June 2011. Web. <http://www.springwise.com/tourism_travel/marriottgame/>.

O'Dell, Jolie. "Are We Too Obsessed With Facebook? [INFOGRAPHIC]." *Mashable.* Mashable, Inc., 12 Jan. 2011. Web. <http://mashable.com/2011/01/12/obsessed-with-facebook-infographic/>.

One Minute on Facebook. *Time Video.* Time Inc. Web. 5 Mar. 2012. <http://www.time.com/time/video/player/0,32068,711054024001_2037229,00.html>

Orenstein, Peggy. "Why Parents Lie to Let Kids Join Facebook." Web log post. *The New York Times: Motherlode.* The New York Times Company, 3 Nov. 2011. Web. <http://parenting.blogs.nytimes.com/2011/11/03/why-parents-lie-to-let-kids-join-facebook/>.

Palfrey, John G. *The Public and the Private at the United States Border with Cyberspace.* [Oxford, MS]: Mississippi Law Journal, 2008. Print.

Palfrey, John G., and Urs Gasser. *Born Digital: Understanding the First Generation of Digital Natives.* New York: Basic, 2008. Print.

Palfrey, John, Urs Gasser, Miriam Simun, and Rosalie Fay Barnes. "Youth, Creativity, and Copyright in the Digital Age." *International Journal of Learning and Media* 1.2 (2009): 79-97. Print.

Palmquist, Matt. "Researchers Tackle the 'Hipster' Phenomenon." *Miller-McCune Magazine* 29 Oct. 2010. Web. <http://www.miller-mccune.com/culture-society/researchers-tackle-the-hipster-phenomenon-24863/>.

Pan, Joann. "Social Media Campaign Finds Tech Entrepreneur a Bone Marrow Donor." Web log post. *Mashable Social Media.* Mashable, Inc., 19 Jan. 2012. Web. <http://mashable.com/2012/01/19/amit-gupta-finds-donor/>.

Parasuco, Trey. "Hipster." *Urban Dictionary.* Urban Dictionary, 22 Nov. 2007. Web. <http://www.urbandictionary.com/define.php?term=hipster>.

Paul, Pamela. "Does Facebook Make Someone Social Offline?" *The New York Times* . The New York Times Company, 28 Jan. 2011, New York ed. The New York Times. 30 Jan. 2011. Web. <http://www.nytimes.com/2011/01/30/fashion/30Studied.html>.

Penn, Mark J., and E. Kinney. Zalesne. *Microtrends: The Small Forces behind Tomorrow's Big Changes.* New York: Twelve, 2007. Print.

Plevin, Julia. "Who's a Hipster?" *The Huffington Post.* TheHuffingtonPost.com, Inc., 8 Aug. 2008. Web. <http://www.huffingtonpost.com/julia-plevin/whos-a-hipster_b_117383.html>.

Popiel, Kat. "Intel's Museum of Me Connects Your Facebook Data to Create a Virtual Exhibit About You." Web log post. *PSFK*. 9 June 2011. Web. <http://www.psfk.com/2011/06/intels-museum-of-me-connects-your-facebook-data-to-create-a-virtual-exhibit-about-you.html>.

Postmes, Tom, and Jolanda Jetten. *Individuality and the Group Advances in Social Identity.* London: SAGE, 2006. Print.

Postrel, Virginia I. *The Substance of Style: How the Rise of Aesthetic Value Is Remaking Commerce, Culture, and Consciousness.* New York: HarperCollins, 2003. Print.

Potter, Andrew. *The Authenticity Hoax: How We Got Lost Finding Ourselves.* [New York]: Harper/HarperCollins, 2010. Print.

Pratt, Andrew. "Email Overload in the Workplace: A Multi-Dimensional Exploration." *Orange Journal.* EServer, 9 Jan. 2006. Web. <http://orange.eserver.org/issues/5-1/pratt.html>.

Qualman, Erik. "10 WOW Social Media Statistics." *Socialnomics.* 7 June 2011. Web. <http://www.socialnomics.net/2011/06/07/10-wow-social-media-statistics/>.

Radicati, Sara. *Email Statistics Report, 2010-2014.* Rep. The Radicati Group, Inc., 19 Apr. 2010. Web. <http://www.radicati.com/?p=5290>.

Rosen, Jeffrey. "The Web Means the End of Forgetting." *The New York Times.* The New York Times Company, 21 July 2010. Web. <http://www.nytimes.com/2010/07/25/magazine/25privacy-t2.html>.

Rosenbaum, Steve. "Why Content Curation Is Here to Stay." *Mashable.* Mashable, Inc., 3 May 2010. Web. <http://mashable.com/2010/05/03/content-curation-creation/>.

Rubin, Sylvia. "Invasion of the Teletubbies." *San Francisco Chronicle* 30 Mar. 1998. Web. <http://www.sfgate.com/cgi-bin/article.cgi?f=/c/a/1998/03/30/DD75322.DTL>.

Sagert, Kelly Boyer. *Flappers: A Guide to an American Subculture.* Santa Barbara, CA: Greenwood, 2010. Print.

Sanders, Tim. *The Likeability Factor: How to Boost Your L-factor & Achieve Your Life's Dreams.* New York: Crown, 2005. Print.

Sann, Paul. *The Lawless Decade; a Pictorial History of a Great American Transition: From the World War I Armistice and Prohibition to Repeal and the New Deal.* New York: Crown, 1957. Print.

Sawers, Paul. "Home, Sweet Home: 60% of UK Employees Could Be Working Remotely within a Decade." *The Next Web.* 22 Feb. 2012. Web. <http://thenextweb.com/uk/2012/02/22/home-sweet-home-60-of-uk-employees-could-be-working-remotely-within-a-decade/>.

Schmidt, Eric. "Technology Is Making Marketing Accountable." Speech. *Google.* Association of National Advertisers, 8 Oct. 2005. Web. <http://www.google.com/press/podium/ana.html>.

Schwartz, Barry. *The Paradox of Choice: Why More Is Less.* New York: HarperCollins, 2004. Print.

Sharp, John. "Top 10 Statistics on Online Dating." *Man Vs. Date.* 28 Jan. 2011. Web. <http://manvsdate.com/top-10-statistics-online-dating/>.

Silverman, Julia. "Yarn Bombers Have a Blast in Portland." *OregonLive. com.* Oregon Live LLC, 9 Sept. 2010. Web. <http://www.oregonlive.com/portland/index.ssf/2010/09/yarn_bombers_have_a_blast_in_p.html>.

Sirius, R. U., and Dan Joy. *Counterculture through the Ages: From Abraham to Acid House.* New York: Villard, 2005. Print.

Skinner, Curtis, Vanessa R. Wight, Yumiko Aratani, Janice L. Cooper, and Kalyani Thampi. *English Language Proficiency, Family Economic Security, and Child Development.* Publication. National Center for Children in Poverty, June 2010. Web. <http://www.nccp.org/publications/pub_948.html>.

Smith, JR. "Kids Are Learning Computer Skills before Life Skills." Web log post. *View from the Top.* AVG Official Blogs, 19 Jan. 2011. Web. <http://blogs.avg.com/view-from-the-top/kids-learning-computer-skills-before-life-skills/>.

Smith, JR. "Would You Want a Digital Footprint from Birth?" Web log post. *View from the Top.* AVG Official Blogs, 6 Oct. 2010. Web. <http://blogs.avg.com/view-from-the-top/would-you-want-a-digital-footprint-from-birth/>.

Springer Science+Business Media. "Children Now Enjoy More Freedom At Home, But Are More Restricted Outside The Home." *ScienceDaily*, 4 Aug. 2009. Web. 2 Mar. 2012.

Staples, Inc. There's No Place Like a Home Office: Staples Survey Shows Telecommuters Are Happier and Healthier, With 25% Less Stress When Working from Home. 19 July 2011. Web. <http://staples. newshq.businesswire.com/press-release/corporate/there%E2%80%99s-no-place-home-office-staples-survey-shows-telecommuters-are-happier-#ixzz1UBEqvM86>.

Steel Magnolias. Dir. Herbert Ross. Perf. Sally Field, Dolly Parton, Julia Roberts, Daryl Hannah, Olympia Dukakis, Shirley MacLaine, Tom Skerritt, and Sam Shepard. Tri-Star, 1989. DVD.

Stelter, Brian, and Jennifer Preston. "Turning to Social Networks for News." *The New York Times.* The New York Times Company, 2 May 2011. Web. <http://www.nytimes.com/2011/05/03/business/media/03media.html>.

Stevens, Kate. *Freak Nation: A Field Guide to 101 of the Most Odd, Extreme, and Outrageous American Subcultures.* Avon, MA: Adams Media, 2010. Print.

Stillman, Jessica. "Scientists Prove Telecommuting Is Awesome." Web log post. *GigaOM.* 14 Nov. 2011. Web. <http://gigaom.com/collaboration/scientists-prove-telecommuting-is-awesome/>.

Strohecker, David P. "Facial Tattoos, A New Form of Distinction." Web log post. *Sociological Images.* The Society Pages, 25 Feb. 2011. Web. <http://thesocietypages.org/socimages/2011/02/25/guest-post-facial-tattoos-a-new-form-of-distinction-2/>.

Surowiecki, James. "In Praise of Distraction." *The New Yorker* 11 Apr. 2011. Web. <http://www.newyorker.com/talk/financial/2011/04/11/110411ta_talk_surowiecki>.

Tapscott, Don. *Grown up Digital: How the Net Generation Is Changing Your World.* New York: McGraw-Hill, 2009. Print.

Teiford, Jenifer B. *Social Perception: 21st Century Issues and Challenges.* New York: Nova Science, 2008. Print.

The Big Lebowski. Dir. Ethan Coen and Joel Coen. Perf. Jeff Bridges, John Goodman and Julianne Moore. Polygram Filmed Entertainment, 1998. DVD.

The Legend of Leigh Bowery. Dir. Charles Atlas. Perf. Leigh Bowery. Atlas Films, 2002. DVD.

The Pennsylvania State University "Tweeting Is More than Just Self-expression." *Penn State Live.* The Pennsylvania State University, 10 Sept. 2009. Web. <http://live.psu.edu/story/41446>.

The Sherman Brothers. "It's a Small World." It's a Small World. 1963. MP3.

Thermidor. "Hip to Be Square: The Failure of Pop Irony." *Everything2.* Everything2 Media, LLC, 13 Dec. 2002. Web. <http://everything2. com/node/1401320>.

Thompson, Elise. "Why Does Everyone Hate (Hipsters) Assholes?" *LAist.* 20 Feb. 2008. Web. <http://laist.com/2008/02/20/why_does_everyo.php>.

U.S. Bureau of Labor Statistics. Division of Labor Force Statistics. *Employee Tenure Summary. Bureau of Labor Statistics.* 14 Sept. 2010. Web. <http://www.bls.gov/news.release/tenure.nr0.htm>.

Ungerleider, Neal. "Wannabe SEALs Help U.S. Navy Hunt Pirates In Massively Multiplayer Game." *Fast Company.* Mansueto Ventures, LLC, 10 May 2011. Web. <http://www.fastcompany.com/1752574/the-us-navys-massively-multiplayer-pirate-hunting-game>.

University of Michigan. "Friends with cognitive benefits: Mental function improves after certain kinds of socializing." *ScienceDaily,* 28 Oct. 2010. Web. <http://www.sciencedaily.com/releases/2010/10/101028113817. htm>.

Weedon, Chris. *Identity and Culture: Narratives of Difference and Belonging.* Maidenhead: Open UP, 2009. Print.

Williams, Alex. "Quality Time, Redefined." *The New York Times.* The New York Times Company, 29 Apr. 2011. Web. <http://www.nytimes. com/2011/05/01/fashion/01FAMILY.html>.

Wilson, David. "More Than Half of Facebook Users Need Their Dose Daily: Chart of the Day." *Bloomberg.* Bloomberg L.P., 2 Feb. 2012. Web. <http://www.bloomberg.com/news/2012-02-03/facebook-turns-into-daily-habit-for-more-users-chart-of-the-day.html>.

Wollan, Malia. "Graffiti's Cozy, Feminine Side." *The New York Times.* The New York Times Company, 18 May 2011. Web. <http://www.nytimes.com/2011/05/19/fashion/creating-graffiti-with-yarn.html>.

Zax, David. "This Is Your Brain on Facebook." *Fast Company.* Mansueto Ventures, LLC, 2 Mar. 2011. Web. <http://www.fastcompany.com/1733483/this-is-your-brain-on-facebook>.

Zuckerberg, Mark. "200 Million Strong." Web log post. *The Facebook Blog.* Facebook, 8 Apr. 2009. Web. <http://blog.facebook.com/blog.php?post=72353897130>.

INDEX

ABOUT THE AUTHOR

Once upon a time, Sophy Bot was leading a yuppie existence on New York's Upper East Side before one day waking up and deciding to change everything all at once—quitting her job, ending her marriage, getting rid of all her belongings and drastically changing her appearance. That was when Bot began exploring the world as a savvy globetrotter and strategic busi-  ness consultant, inadvertently picking up the "hipster" label somewhere along the way. Whether she's buttoned up in freshly pressed slacks or rocking a giraffe-print vest, Bot now leads a seamless coexistence in both the corporate and creative worlds, offering a rare interpretation of the modern hipster from both the inside and out. Sophy Bot currently lives in northern California with her handsome pup, Banksy, but has been known to change locations several times a year.

To connect with Bot and the Hipster Effect online, visit thehipstereffect.com or follow @hipstereffect on Twitter.

Inquiries delivered via carrier pigeon will receive priority.

13112067R00117

Printed in Great Britain
by Amazon.co.uk, Ltd.,
Marston Gate.